THE YOUNG GREEN CONSUMER GUIDE

John Elkington and Julia Hailes
With Douglas Hill
Illustrations by Tony Ross

GUILD PUBLISHING
LONDON · NEW YORK · SYDNEY · TORONTO

Contents

Glossary 4

Helping to Save the Earth 6

THE ISSUES

The Greenhouse Effect 8

Holes in the Ozone Layer 10

Acid Rain 12

Destroying the Rainforests 14

How do you Find the Energy? 16

Getting About 18

Farming the Land 22

Water, Water Everywhere 24

Save the Animals 26

Mountains of Waste 28

AT HOME

The Bathroom 32

The Kitchen 35

The Sitting Room 51

The Bedroom 53

How Green is Your Home? 58

AT SCHOOL 60

First things first 63

The Classroom 66

Food and drink 67

The Grounds 69

Cleaning 70

Rubbish 71

Travelling 72

Saving energy and water 73

The Neighbourhood 75

MAKING AND DOING 76

Organisations You Can Join 86

Useful Addresses 88

Other Books to Read 91

Index 93

Glossary

Acid rain Acid rain contains chemicals washed out of the sky—including sulphur dioxide and nitrogen oxide. These are produced whenever we burn fossil fuels to produce energy. Acid rain—and acid mists and fogs—can cause serious damage to lakes, trees and buildings.

Biodegradable A substance is biodegradable if it can be broken down by bacteria and other biological means into carbon dioxide and water.

Catalytic converter A gadget which can be built into cars and which cleans up most of the poisonous fumes in the exhaust—but not carbon dioxide.

Chlorofluorocarbons (CFCs) A family of extremely useful chemicals, found in such products as aerosols, foam plastics, fridges and air conditioners. Unfortunately, CFCs are now known to be destroying the ozone layer.

Deforestation The clearing of forests by felling, burning or overgrazing. This is particularly serious in tropical regions. *See* RAINFOREST.

Ecology The study of the interactions between living organisms and their environment.

Ecosystem Whether it's a coral reef or a rainforest, an ecosystem is a living system embracing air, water, soils, plants and animals. Food and energy pass around an

ecosystem in cycles or loops, so each part of the system depends on many others.

Energy The force behind heat, light and movement. Fuel is required to produce energy: food for humans, petrol for cars, electricity (produced from coal, gas, oil, the sun, the wind and more) for everything from cookers to computers.

Energy conservation This involves cutting down your use of anything which needs energy to work. At its simplest, energy conservation means switching off the lights when you leave a room.

Energy efficiency To achieve improved energy efficiency, buildings and equipment (factories, cars, homes, light-bulbs) must be designed to produce more of what we want (heat, light, movement and so on) for the energy used.

Environment The surroundings in which we and other living organisms live. In the country, much of the environment is natural or semi-natural; in our towns and cities most of it is man-made.

Fossil fuels These include coal, oil and gas. They began to form millions of years ago when sediment covered plant and animal matter, which then broke down under conditions of pressure and heat. Because they take such a long time to form, fossil fuels are effectively NON RENEWABLE.

ee-range Whether they are chickens or ws, free-range animals are reared in nditions which allow them to move out outside—rather than being con-ually cooped up.

eenhouse Effect The warming of the mosphere produced by the build-up of ses, chiefly carbon dioxide, in the rth's atmosphere. The gases trap the at of the sun. The levels of carbon diox-e, methane, nitrous oxides and CFCs ee above) now being produced are ought to be producing a 'global warm-g' trend.

on-renewable resource A resource that, ice formed, does not replace itself. ving resources (grass, trees or fish) tend be renewable, whereas FOSSIL FUELS d other mineral resources (coal, oil, gas metals) are non-renewable.

rganic farming Farming which respects e health of the soil and environment. rganic farmers use manures and com-st, coupled with natural forms of pest ntrol, rather than synthetic chemicals r fertilizers or pesticides.

zone layer A layer of ozone (O_3), 20–50 n above the earth's surface, which pro-cts all living organisms from an over-se of the sun's ultraviolet rays.

llution Something that is foul, filthy or rty somewhere that we do not think it is sirable.

Rainforest Dense forest—often called 'jungle'—found in tropical areas where there is heavy rainfall. These forests, which are among the richest reservoirs of species in the world, often grow on very poor soils. If destroyed, they may leave only desert behind.

Recycling Breaking down waste (e.g. glass, metals, plastics, paper or kitchen waste) so that it can be made into some-thing else (e.g. bottles, cans, plastic, pa-per, garden compost).

Renewable energy Energy from sources which will not run out, because they are powered by the sun, wind, waves, tides or underground (geothermal) heat.

Re-usable Something (e.g. a milk bottle or egg box) that can be used a number of times before its materials are recycled, burned to recover energy, or simply thrown away.

Third World A term often used to de-scribe the poorer countries of Africa, South America and Asia.

Waste disposal Ideally, waste should be recycled or re-used wherever possible. More often, however, it is dumped in holes in the ground (landfill) or at sea, or it is burnt (incineration).

Helping to Save the Earth

From Manchester to Moscow, from Tokyo to Toronto, young people like you are more aware than ever that our world is under threat.

You almost certainly watch more television than your parents. This means that you probably know more about some of the key environmental issues—the hole in the ozone layer, the destruction of the rainforests, the Greenhouse Effect—than they, and many of your teachers, do.

If you feel that you want to know even more—and you want to know how we can find solutions—then we have written this book for you. In particular, we have set out to show what *you* can do to help create a cleaner, greener world.

Everybody can do *something*, and what we do now counts more than at any other time in history. Many more changes have taken place in this century than ever before and they have come about faster than at any previous time in our history. Inventions that were the stuff of science fiction have become an everyday reality. Ask your parents if they knew about the things on this list when they were young:

aircraft hijacks	dishwashers
answering	dry roasted nuts
machines	filofaxes
black plastic sacks	home computers
BMX bikes	jumbo jets
cassette tapes	oven chips
colour TV	pound coins
Concorde	ring-pull cans
digital phones	videos
digital watches	Walkmans

Some of the changes have improved our way of life, but they have also meant that our lifestyles are beginning to threaten the existence of the planet. Our methods of making things, using them and throwing them away are affecting not just the birds, the insects and the other animals but also the air we breathe and the water we drink.

Suddenly people are realising that we cannot ignore the threat. We need to do something—and many people are. Many are becoming 'green consumers'.

Are you a green consumer?
As a green consumer you should be trying to avoid things likely to:

- Harm your health, or the health of others.

- Significantly damage the environment whilst being made, used or thrown away.

- Create unnecessary waste, either because they use too much packaging or because they will be quickly thrown away.

- Use materials which come from animals, plants or places which are threatened with destruction.

- Involve the unnecessary use of—or cruelty to—animals.

- Cause people to suffer in other countries, particularly in the poorer countries of the 'Third World'.

You will be surprised how much power you have as a green consumer. Once you start to choose between those things which harm our environment and those which are less damaging, you will be forcing the makers of harmful goods to change their methods. If they don't change, and if you still refuse to use their brands, then they risk going out of business.

One of the most effective ways you can use your power is by talking to people. Parents listen to their children much more than you might think. You can also help to make your teachers, your school friends and other people as green as you!

One of the best ways to make changes happen is to ask questions and this book is full of suggestions. You will be able to think of many more—about the products you buy, about the food you eat, about the clothes you wear, about the buildings and transport you use. Many people won't know the answers to your questions at first. But maybe they *should* know. Sometimes they will simply not have thought of the issue before and your question may be just the spur they need to start thinking—and then to do something about it.

And don't be put off by people who just see you as a nuisance. The more you know about what is happening, the more you can change things.

The Earth's problems won't go away without your help, and what you do *will* make a difference.

Think of all the living things in the world joined in a long chain. The trees, the air, the water, plants, insects and animals—including people—rely on each other as part of an ecosystem. We could not survive very long with poisoned air, poisoned water, and no animals or plants. Even if some of the problems seem a long way away, anything that affects the chain will affect us in the end.

One of the greatest problems for the Earth is that the human population is increasing very rapidly and, if we don't change now, more and more people will cause more and more damage. But it is also a world of young people—by some point in the 1990s more than half the people in the world will be under 20.

So becoming a young green consumer is very important. Try out some of the ideas we have come up with, and think up your own. Persuade your school to carry out an 'environmental audit' (see page 60). We look forward to hearing how you get on!

Our address is: John Elkington and Julia Hailes, SustainAbility Ltd, 49 Princes Place, London W11 4QA.

The Greenhouse Effect

It's easy to understand the Greenhouse Effect by thinking of the greenhouse in a garden. If you have one, or there is one nearby, try sitting in it on a sunny day. Feel the sun shining through the glass. Feel it warming up the air, warming up the earth and the plants that grow in it. The glass is doing two things. It is letting the sunshine in—and preventing much of the warmth escaping. So the greenhouse is a heat trap.

Now imagine the Earth inside a kind of greenhouse with the atmosphere around it acting like the glass, letting sunlight in while keeping much of the warmth from getting out. Atmosphere is essential to all living things and without it the Earth would be as cold and lifeless as the surface of the moon. The trouble is that our atmosphere is changing because we are polluting it with chemicals—in the form of gases—and it is keeping in too *much* heat.

Invisible gases
You can't see the gases as they drift up into the atmosphere, but they are on of the worst threats facing the environment. The most important greenhouse gas is *carbon dioxide* (CO_2) Humans produce it every time w breathe out, but there's nothing w can do about that! The main source o CO_2 pollution is the burning of fossi fuels—e.g. coal, oil, petrol—and wood.

Other greenhouse gases are *nitroger oxide*, given off by cars as we driv them and by coal-burning powe stations, *methane*, produced when animals (and humans!) fart, and by rotting plants, and *chlorofluorocarbon* (CFCs) which we'll come across late (see page 10).

We have been living with most o these gases for a long time, but we'r now producing too many of them They are building up in the atmos phere and allowing too little of th

un's heat to escape into space. This process of overheating is called 'global warming'. The change so far is so small that it's hardly noticeable—but it is happening.

Some people, especially those living in northern countries such as Britain and Scandinavia, think it would be nice to have their chilly weather warmed up. However, if the temperature were to rise by only a few more degrees a number of things would happen:

- Some of the ice around the North and South Poles would melt.

- Sea levels would rise.

- The weather would begin to change.

Some scientists now think that the average sea level could rise by nearly two metres by the middle of the next century. The results of this would be catastrophic. Throughout the world, many coastal areas would simply vanish beneath the waves. Low-lying countries, such as Bangladesh (which already suffers dreadful floods) and Holland, would disappear. Great cities—London, New York and Tokyo among them—would be drowned. Seawater would surge up the rivers,

and the salt would kill many of the things which live in and around the water.

Hundreds of different living creatures could become extinct, while many kinds of pests (such as rats and mosquitoes) would flourish in the warmer climate.

Europe could be hit by tropical storms and hurricanes. Food might be a problem, too. At the moment nations such as Britain import a great deal of their food from other countries—but many of those countries may not have food to spare if large areas of farmland are flooded, ruined by seawater or affected by drought.

YGC
Action

One way to help:

Cut down on the electricity you use and you cut down on the CO_2 produced by power stations. So turn off the lights and the electric fire when you're not using them. And don't keep reboiling the electric kettle for one cup of tea!

Earth's natural solutions

Just as some of the greenhouse gases are produced naturally, so some of them are soaked up naturally. Sea-water soaks up carbon dioxide—and so do the enormous growths of tiny organisms in the sea, called plankton. However, plankton take up more CO_2 in colder water. So as the Greenhouse Effect warms up the world and the oceans with it, worryingly, the plankton absorb less carbon dioxide.

Land plants soak up carbon dioxide as well, especially the trees in the mighty 'rainforests' of the tropics. But they are being destroyed by felling and burning. What's more, the burning actually produces enormous volumes of CO_2 and so adds to the problem. Rainforest burning is one of the greatest contributors to the Greenhouse Effect. (See page 14.)

It's already here

Many scientists say that the Greenhouse Effect has already started to affect us. They point to odd changes in the weather, among them the recent mild winters and warm summers of drought in North America, turning the vast sweep of wheat-growing prairies into dust; and the discovery in 1987 of tropical sea creatures in the supposedly cold waters around Britain, including the triggerfish found off Devon and Cornwall.

Holes in the Ozone Layer

Ozone is an invisible gas, a form of oxygen. It occurs 20–50 km (10–30 miles) above the ground, and forms a protective layer around the Earth that we desperately need. Without it the sun would frazzle us.

The ozone layer shields us from one particular part of sunlight, ultra-violet (UV) light. Enough UV light gets through to give people their sun-tans—but if much more of it were allowed to filter through, it would cause a number of problems. These include eye and skin diseases, damage to crops, and to fish and the plankton they feed on.

Chlorofluorocarbons (CFCs)

We are damaging the ozone layer with a family of chemicals called chloro-fluorocarbons, pronounced *kloro-floro-karbons*. CFCs have been used in a number of ways, including the manufacture of egg boxes, takeaway

hamburger boxes and foam-filled furniture. They do most of the cooling in refrigerators and air conditioners, and are used to clean the chip boards that erve as the memory in modern computers.

Scientists are beginning to develop other, less harmful products. Until recently, for example, when you sprayed most aerosol cans you sprayed out CFCs along with the contents (hairspray, deodorant, shaving foam etc). The CFCs were used to help shoot the contents out of the can. Nowadays they have been removed from most aerosols and an alternative propellant is used. These cans are often labelled 'ozone friendly'. There are also alternatives which can be used in hamburger boxes and egg boxes.

No household fridge has yet been made without CFCs, although some are made with fewer. So, while much has been done, we still have a long way to go.

Holes over the Poles
In 1985 scientists realised that the ozone layer was not just thinning,

there was actually a hole over the Antarctic. A very big hole. By 1987 it had stretched to cover an area as large as the USA. In 1988 scientists found another hole, this time over the Arctic. This one stretched over an area the size of Greenland. The holes constantly change shape and size, depending on the time of year.

International concern about the holes was so great that in 1988 nearly 40 countries signed an agreement called the 'Montreal Protocol'. They aimed to cut the use of CFCs by 50% by 1999, and it now looks as though we will switch away from them even sooner.

But some of the poorer countries such as India and China argue that it's unfair for rich countries, who have had such things as fridges and aerosols for years, to limit the use of CFCs just when poorer people are getting to the stage when they can afford them for the first time. It's a good point, but a difficult one. There are one billion people in China. If they all had a fridge using CFCs there would soon be more hole than ozone layer. Perhaps we in the rich countries should be providing money to help others afford the more costly alternatives to CFCs.

**YGC
Action**

One way to help preserve the ozone layer is to make sure that if a new fridge is bought it is one of the new reduced-CFC models. And try to discourage anyone who is thinking of buying a car with an air conditioning system.

Acid Rain

In the 19th century, it was noticed that some plants and trees in Britain were suffering a 'blight'. A man named Angus Smith investigated, found the cause and gave it a name that we still use. Acid rain.

At that time huge amounts of coal were burned in Britain in hundreds of factories. Today, even more coal is burned all over the world, especially in power stations producing electri-city. We also burn other 'fossil fuels' — petrol in cars and gas and oil for cooking and heating. All this sends smoke and fumes into the air. Burning coal produces a gas called sulphur dioxide. Burning petrol and natural gas produces nitrogen oxide. The sulphur dioxide and nitrogen oxide mix with water droplets in the clouds and come back to earth as sulphuric acid and nitric acid in the rain—acid rain.

Killer rain

Acid rain may not burn human skin, but for plants and fish it's a killer. Fish were starting to disappear from European lakes in the 1930s. By the 1960s and '70s vast numbers had died. And obviously this has affected the water-side creatures dependent on fish as their food source.

But this isn't just a sad story about dead wildlife. Rivers and lakes are important sources of income and food for people. Acid rain is putting an end to that. It also kills trees. Half of West Germany's woodlands — including the mighty Black Forest—are dying; a third of Switzerland's; 40% of Holland's. Millions of acres in Austria and Czechoslovakia are suffering. And in Britain, too, forests have been found to be seriously damaged by acid rain.

Buildings and monuments are also affected. Many are being slowly eaten

away. When acid rain attacked buildings in Montreal, Canada, in the mid-1980s, it was said to turn the stone into a spongy mass 'that could be cut like cheese'.

Britain causes a great deal of this acid rain. British power stations give off more sulphur than many of the other European nations put together. But other countries produce it too. Most of the acid rain produced by Americans falls on their neighbours in Canada. Canadian lakes are dying; Canadian trees are dying. Even the sugar maple tree, the country's national emblem, has been severely affected.

Now the European nations are taking action to reduce acid rain. But progress will take time, and an amazing amount of money.

Believe it or not
Sweden has about 4,000 lakes with virtually no fish at all, while another 20,000 are rapidly going that way. (Sweden has a great many lakes.) Acid rain is the culprit.

Destroying the Rainforests

The rainforests grow in a belt around the Equator. They thrive in hot climates. The largest is the Amazonian rainforest, in Brazil, but there are others in Africa, in Asia, and even as far south as Australia.

The rainforests are home to millions of plants, animals, birds and insects. We haven't even discovered most of them yet. Each of these species plays its part in the ecosystem—the intricate web of life in which every living thing depends upon many others.

But the rainforests are vanishing. Many have suffered from uncontrolled felling or burning. This happens for a number of reasons:

- Much of the wood from the trees (such as mahogany and teak) is valuable. It is sold to people in richer countries who then make all sorts of things from it—furniture, window frames, loo seats, saucepan handles and even throwaway chopsticks! This wood is called 'tropical hardwood'.

- The forest is burned to make room for housing and farming, needed by the rapidly growing human populations.

- Land is cleared to turn it into pasture for beef cattle. They are reared for their meat, some of which will be made into hamburgers and tinned beef and sold in faraway countries.

- Sometimes the land is flooded to make hydro-electric dams to provide electricity.

In 1988, more Brazilian rainforest was destroyed than at any other time in history. If the destruction continues at this rate, every tree in the immensity of Amazonia will be gone within 3 years. It is a difficult problem to solve however, partly because many rainforest countries such as Brazil owe colossal sums of money to other richer countries—America and the European nations for example. Brazil therefore sells its wood and meat to help pay its debts.

What happens when rainforests are destroyed?

- Trees soak up carbon dioxide, so by burning and felling so many of them we are destroying one of our most vital defences against the Greenhouse Effect.

- The burning of the forests sends massive amounts of carbon dioxide into the atmosphere, making the Greenhouse Effect ever worse.

YGC Action

One way to help save the rainforests is to avoid using tropical hardwood in your home. Check to see whether any has been used for your window frames, doors, loo seats and saucepan handles. And eat brazil nuts! (See page 40.)

- No longer held in place by tree roots, large amounts of soil are washed away by rain. This is called soil erosion. The soil runs into the rivers, clogging them and causing them to flood. Whole villages and towns can be flooded—and, in the case of Bangladesh, almost the whole country.

- Very few plants can grow in place of the trees because the rain washes away all the good things, the nutrients, from the land.

- Wildlife of every kind dies when the tropical forests go. There are some species which can only live in the rainforest, so they are gone for ever—tigers, birds, monkeys, butterflies, gorillas and many, many more.

Believe it or not
The Japanese throw away 16 million pairs of chopsticks every day—all of them made from the precious wood from the tropical rainforests of Sarawak.

- Some of the plants in the rainforest are used to make medicines. By destroying the forests we are destroying a potential medicine cabinet which may hold cures for cancer, AIDS and other deadly diseases.

- The rainforest is also home to peoples whose ways of life are disappearing, together with their valuable knowledge about what is to be found in these forests.

How do you Find the Energy?

When we talk in this book about using energy at home and school, we don't mean the energy in your body but the gas, oil and electricity we use for light and heat. These energy forms pose a number of environmental problems.

- Gas and oil are both fossil fuels and contribute to the Greenhouse Effect and to acid rain when they are burnt. They are not, however, as damaging as coal.

- Some people have coal fires at home but, more importantly, many power stations run by burning coal and it is the power stations which supply our electricity. So every time we leave a light on unnecessarily, or forget to turn the television off, we're needlessly contributing both to the Greenhouse Effect and acid rain.

Nuclear power
Electricity is also produced in a nuclear reactor. Nuclear power is difficult to understand and people cannot agree whether it's a good thing or a bad thing. It creates nuclear waste (radioactive waste) which remains radioactive—and therefore extremely dangerous to humans and other life—for thousands of years. It is very expensive to find a suitable and safe space to dump the waste. Most people are pretty sure they do not want these nuclear waste dumps to be near where they live!

Nuclear power has also caused some very nasty accidents. The one that happened in Russia when a reactor in a nuclear power station at Chernobyl exploded, affected the *whole of Europe* and large parts of Scandinavia.

Although the production of nuclear energy has one great advantage in environmental terms—it doesn't produce greenhouse gases—it is very expensive and difficult to make it safe and some scientists are doing their best to find alternatives.

Alternative energy
There are many other, less widely used, sources of energy. They are all renewable, to a greater or lesser degree, which means that they will not run out, but each of them can cause its own environmental problems.

- *Solar energy* works by capturing heat from the sun but a solar power plant takes up a great deal of space. For instance, a plant able to produce as much energy as a nuclear reactor might need up to 5,000 acres of land whereas the nuclear plant only needs about 150 acres.

- *Windmills* also take up a great deal of land because so many are needed to produce large amounts of energy. They can also be noisy.

- *Wave power*—using waves to push machinery, air or water in such a way that electricity can be generated—is very difficult to make work.

Tidal power works by building a barrage (a dam) across a river estuary or bay. As the tide rises so does the water behind the dam and electricity can be produced as the water is let out. But one problem is that the dam and the reservoir destroy the habitat of animals and birds.

Geothermal power (heat from the earth) can only be used in a few areas where heat from the earth's core escapes to the surface through geysers and volcanoes. Iceland is one such place. Where there are no natural escape routes for the heat, pipes have to be drilled into the ground, often miles deep. This is expensive and can cause pollution.

Biomass power (taking energy from plants) also needs a great deal of land if the plants have to be specially planted. Up to 125,000 acres would have to be planted to produce the same energy as a nuclear reactor. In Brazil, sugar cane is converted into fuel for cars and gas can also be produced from animal dung and human sewage.

So, although alternative, or renewble, energy does have a useful role to play, we can't expect it to solve all our nergy problems overnight. It won't. The basic message is that we should se as little energy as possible if we

want to help reduce the problems. We can do this by:

- **energy conservation** e.g. turning down the central heating thermostat so that less heat is produced and therefore less energy used.

- **energy efficiency** e.g. using equipment that produces the same amount of heat but uses less energy to do so.

We need both. Whoever we are and whatever we are doing, the real challenge is to do more with less.

YGC Action

One very important way of helping is to make sure your home is energy efficient. (See pages 49 and 51.)

Getting About

If all the cars in the world were parked end to end, they would stretch around the equator over 36 times—and that is not counting lorries, vans, buses or motorbikes! Just the cars in London would form a monster traffic jam piled ten cars high stretching from John O'Groats to Land's End.

All choked up and nowhere to go

We travel much more—and much further—than our grandparents ever did, and whereas they used to travel by bus, train, boat or even horse and cart, we are much more likely to go by car or by plane.

Most people prefer to travel by car—it is generally more convenient and it will take you door to door. They may also have little choice because bus and train services are often poor, expensive and unreliable. The situation is made worse the more we become accustomed to using cars because cities nowadays are built in such a way tha we can only get around them by ca

In England there are about two mi lion new cars on the road every yea and only one and a half million ol ones scrapped. This means half a mi lion *more* every year. More cars mean

- *More metals* have to be mined t manufacture them.

- *More energy* is needed to run th mines and factories.

- *More ugly, wasteful scrap heaps.*

- *More pollution from exhaust pipes* Petrol engines produce nitroge oxides which cause acid rain, ca bon monoxide (which is what kil people when they breathe in ex haust fumes), carbon dioxide (th major greenhouse gas) and hydro carbons. Old diesel engines, o

the other hand, often produce clouds of sooty smoke—and a great deal of noise! Buses, taxis and lorries often use diesel—it is not much fun to follow them if you are on a bike.

- *More accidents.* You may well have seen a road accident, probably a small one, and you will most likely have seen TV reports of big crashes that can kill many people at once. But you may not realise just how many people are killed or injured on British roads every year. In 1988, for example, 99,587 car drivers were killed or injured, 71,118 passengers and 25,849 cyclists. That same year, 41,050 children were killed or injured in road accidents!

- *More traffic jams.* One day in 1989, Britain experienced a 130-km (80-mile) jam! Cities like Rome have been trying to control the number of cars by only allowing even-number-plated cars into the city on one day and odd-numbered the next.

- *More land is used up.* Every km of motorway puts around 6.5 hectares of land under concrete and tarmac. In the 1980s, Britain built 430 km (270 miles) of motorway, which means that about 2,800 hectares (7,000 acres) were concreted over.

- *More fuel is used.* Finally there is the sheer quantity of petrol and other fuels which we get through every year—30 billion litres (6.8 billion gallons) of petrol and 11 billion litres (2.4 billion gallons) of diesel for road transport alone. Although the North Sea has provided the majority of our oil for the last ten years and more, all the signs are that this source is heading for 'Empty'.

Cars are not the only problem—lorries are an environmental headache too. Ever-larger lorries storm through our cities, towns and villages. They damage bridges, roads and buildings, and the noise they produce makes many people's lives a misery.

Unleaded route
Of course it has not all been bad news. You probably know that unleaded petrol is now widely available. Lead is highly poisonous. In large quantities it can damage the brain and nerves, particularly of children because they are still growing.

YGC Action

Use trains and buses, walk or cycle whenever you can and if you travel by car check that it uses unleaded petrol. Make sure anyone buying a new car chooses a fuel-efficient model (runs a long way on one litre of petrol) with a catalytic converter.

Using unleaded is therefore a step in
the right direction. It also opens the
way for catalytic converters—gadgets
which clean up exhaust fumes and
which can only work on cars using
unleaded petrol. In America, most cars
have catalytic converters and they
are becoming much more common in
Europe, too.

Catalytic converters reduce the pollution which causes acid rain and
smog. Unfortunately, however, they
do not cut down on the amount of
carbon dioxide, so the car will still
contribute to the Greenhouse Effect.
Also, catalytic converters are made
with rare metals, the mining of which
can cause destruction of rainforests
and other environmental damage.

Better to fly?

It may seem, with all the problems
caused by cars, that flying must be
better. Unfortunately not. Aeroplanes
use an enormous amount of fuel. Even
if you take into account that some of
them can carry lots of passengers, and
that they travel a long way very fast,
the amount of fuel needed for each
passenger is very large.

It is important to remember that
aeroplanes use more fuel the mor
weight they carry. Every poun
makes a difference. A single intercor
tinental 747 Jumbo, for example, ca
save fuel worth £12,000 in one yea
by serving drinks from light plasti
bottles rather than glass ones!

Planes also get caught in traffic jam
and often have to queue to land. Som
are left circling airports for hours. A
the time gobbling fuel and producin
fumes.

Trains then

Yes, trains are a good option. If you
take into account the number of pas
sengers they can carry and the numbe
of miles they travel, trains turn out to
use fuel very efficiently. There are
other benefits, too. Fewer roads, less
traffic, less pollution.

You might think, therefore, tha
more railways than roads would be
built. Unfortunately not. In most
countries, thousands of miles of *roads*

have been built since World War II, but the railways have either been cut back or, at best, expanded by only a few miles. And when the railways are very popular, and lots of people use them, the fares are often increased to put people off and stop the trains getting so crowded! Why not put on *more* trains instead?

Buses too
Although buses cause pollution and traffic congestion, they are still better than cars. More people can fit into one vehicle and so each passenger individually is contributing less to such problems as noise, air pollution and traffic jams.

Bicycles
The best machine for the environment is the bicycle. 1600 km on a

thimbleful of oil, no noise, no need for motorways ripping the country apart. There is even the bonus of healthy exercise for the rider.

Unfortunately, cycling is not always practical since nowadays we often want to travel long distances. It is also made difficult by all the other

road traffic.
But often it is only habit that induces us to go by car rather than make the most of a bike.

Make sure you know how to ride one safely and use it, if you are allowed to, for visiting friends, going to school and for local journeys.

Farming the Land

The variety and quantity of foods available in the shops has increased dramatically in the last 20 years. Ask your parents if they ever had corn on the cob, avocados or mangoes when they were children. One reason for the change is that more food is imported from distant countries but another is that farmers are growing much more on their land now.

They have been helped by chemicals (fertilizers) which top up the nutrients in the soil, making it more productive.

Other chemicals (herbicides and pesticides) are used to protect crops from weeds, pests and tiny fungi. Hormones and antibiotics are often fed to farm animals to keep them healthy and speed up their growth.

There are a number of environmental problems linked to all these chemicals. Artificial fertilizers can become part of a vicious circle. They enable farmers to grow more crops but this means that the soil's natural goodness is quickly used up and is not replaced. The farmer must therefore spread more and more fertilizer to keep the crops growing strongly. When it rains the fertilizer soaks into the soil or runs off into rivers where it can damage plants and creatures. Two groups of chemicals, nitrates and phosphates, make some water plants grow so quickly that they don't leave room for anything else. As the plants rot, they take oxygen out of the water, so even the fish begin to suffocate. Nitrates can get into our drinking water, sometimes in larger amounts than doctors think is good for us. Steps are now being taken to cut down on their use but there is still a long way to go.

Another thing that farmers do to grow more crops is to pull out the hedgerows so that the fields are much larger. This enables them to sow more land and also to use larger machinery for ploughing, planting, spraying and harvesting. But hedges are home to all sorts of wildlife—flowers, birds and small animals—and many of them die when their hedgerow homes are destroyed. And, without the hedges as windbreaks, much of the fertile top soil on the land is blown away.

Factory farming

Factory farming—keeping a great many birds or animals together in one place, usually in confined spaces and without access to daylight—enables farmers to grow more food and to sell it more cheaply but it also causes a number of problems. If one animal or bird has a disease it is passed on very quickly to the others and this encourages the spread of the viruses and bacteria that cause such diseases as salmonella. Also, hundreds of animals in one place produce an enormous amount of dung. Mixed with urine, this is called slurry. Some is used as fertilizer on fields and some is just washed away. Slurry is very strong and when it finds its way into rivers it causes serious pollution.

Organic farming

However, a growing number of farmers, concerned about the effects of chemicals on the environment and on our food, have turned to organic methods. They use natural compost and animal manure to fertilize their fields. They use 'crop rotation' instead of growing the same thing on the same field every year. So they don't wear out the soil or let the numbers of pests which attack a particular crop build up. They don't use chemical sprays, but instead increase the 'natural resistance' of their crops and animals to pests, diseases and so on.

Naturally, there are drawbacks. It takes at least two years before the land can be 'cured' of all the chemicals that had been poured on to it in the past. For those years, a farmer switching to organic farming may earn very little. Also, organic farming means more hand labour for the farmer—or more workers to employ and pay—so the food is more expensive to produce. Partly for these reasons, organic farmers are still hugely outnumbered by the rest.

Believe it or not
Forty-five million hens in Britain are kept in battery cages in order to supply us with eggs.

Water, Water Everywhere

How much water do *you* use?

The water in your home is pumped from rivers and reservoirs. The more water you use, the more likely it is that yet another beautiful valley will have to be flooded as a reservoir, or that another river will begin to run dry, killing the wildlife in and around it. Also, the more dirty water you send down the drain the more difficult it is for the sewage farm to cope. Accidental overflows of sewage can seriously pollute land and water.

It's difficult to imagine how much water is used in your home every day but here's a rough guide.

	litres	gallons
1 flush of the loo	10	2.2
1 bath	80	17.6
1 shower	30	6.6
1 washing-machine load	100	22.0
1 dishwasher load	50	11.0

That's an awful lot of water, and so any way you can find to help save it— like turning off a dripping tap—really will help to protect the environment.

Polluting the rivers

We've already discovered how farming can pollute rivers. So can factories if they're not careful about how they dispose of their waste. But did you know that the ordinary household adds to water pollution every day? Bleach or other strong chemicals poured into the loo to clean it are water pollutants, as are many other household cleaners. (See page 47.) When phosphates, found in most washing powders, find their way into rivers after they've been flushed away from our homes, they can encourage algae in the water to grow very fast and to use up all the oxygen. (See also page 22.) Nowadays, however, there are washing powders in the shops which are phosphate-free.

Polluting the seas

Eventually, all rivers run into the sea taking with them the pollution washed from the fields, factories and cities along their way. During the summer of 1989, pollution from such rivers as the Po in Italy created huge mountains of slimy green algae in the Adriatic Sea between Italy and Yugoslavia. The slime, looking like something from a science fiction film, washed up onto the beaches, much to the surprise of holidaymakers.

But this is only one way in which the oceans are being polluted. They also suffer from the dumping of dangerous chemicals, raw human sewage and radioactive waste from the nuclear industry, as well as from the huge oil slicks which kill birds and marine life after an oil tanker accident. In 1989, a tanker called the *Exxon Valdez* ran aground in the beautiful Prince William Sound, Alaska. Millions of litres of oil gushed out and high winds spread it into a slick stretching for 2,400 km. Whales, seals, otters, polar bears, caribou and seabirds suffered and died. So did the fish on which a large fishing industry depended. It will take years to clean up the mess and the cost will be astronomical. A list of oil spills could go on and on.

In 1988 thousands of seals died in the North Sea and scientists said that pollutants had weakened their resi-

An easy way to help is by saving water. Take a shower instead of a bath (see page 32) and don't leave the taps running while you're brushing your teeth or washing your hands.

stance to disease. We eat great quantities of fish from the North Sea and many people now wonder how much they too are affected by pollution.

There is a huge amount of water in an ocean, so that until recently polluting substances, which were diluted and spread over a wide area, were less harmful. But nowadays we are pumping in so much that some seas—the Baltic, the North Sea and the Mediterranean among them—just can't cope any longer. They can't dilute the poisons quickly enough.

Believe it or not
Britain has 44,000 km (27,500 miles) of rivers and estuaries. 4400 km (2,750 miles) are so dirty that no fish can live in them.

The average family of four uses 3,500 litres (770 gallons) of water every week. One third is used for flushing the loo. More water is used for that than for anything else in the home.

Leaving a garden sprinkler on for one hour uses 910 litres (200 gallons) of water.

Save the Animals

Since humans are the brainiest animals, we are mostly able to make other animals do what we want. And it's not always very good for them.

Buying free-range
The term 'free-range' means that the birds or animals can wander around outside, rather than being cramped up in tiny cages or stalls. Most people know about free-range eggs but you can also buy free-range poultry and meat—beef, lamb and pork.

Buying cruelty-free
All sorts of animals—particularly mice, rats, rabbits and guinea pigs, but also dogs and monkeys—are used every year to test the safety of products which will be used next by human beings. These include shampoos, cosmetics, cleaners and medicines.

Testing the safety of medicines which could save our lives is obviously very important but many people feel that animals should not be used to test things that we don't really need because they often experience considerable pain on our behalf. This is why some companies sell products labelled 'cruelty-free'. This can mean that the product:

- Contains nothing made from animals
  or
- has not been tested on animals
  or
- contains no ingredients that have been tested on animals.

Sometimes, happily, all three are true.

Protecting endangered species
Ever since animals and plants first ap-

...peared on Earth, millions of years ago, he species on the planet have evolved (changed). Some have become extinct t the same time that others have developed. In fact, over 90% of the species that have ever lived on the planet no longer exist. So extinction is natural. The problem is that since humans appeared—a *lot* later than most other life forms—the rate of extinction has speeded up dramatically. Today, many species are threatened because humans consider them—or bits of hem!—particularly valuable or attractive. Elephants are killed for their ivory tusks; rhinos for their horns. Whales are hunted for the oils in their flesh and sharks to make shark-fin soup. Plants such as cyclamen and cacti are threatened because they are sometimes taken from the wild to be sold to plant lovers. There are many more species in danger—certain monkeys, parrots, turtles and tigers—and you probably know others too.

YGC Action

Have a look round your house. Can you find anything that comes from an endangered species? See pages 56 and 57 for some clues. If you're buying toiletries (soap, bubble bath etc.) as a present, look out for those labelled 'cruelty-free'.

Believe it or not

Scientists think that at the beginning of this century the world was losing about one species a year. By the middle of the 1980s we were losing one species a *day* from the 5–10 million in existence.

Mountains of Waste

How many things will you throw away today? The box from a new tube of toothpaste? The empty cereal box or milk carton? Your bus ticket? Perhaps a crisp packet and an empty drink can? Start a list of the things you throw away in one day and you'll be amazed at how long it becomes.

Each year the average British family throws out:

- waste paper which took around six trees to make

- more than 500 cans, of which 300 are food or pet food cans

- 47 kilos of plastics, 32 kilos of metals, 45 kilos of food and 74 kilos of glass.

That means that each of us is throwing away more than ten times our body weight in rubbish every year.

Packaging

Almost one-third of our rubbish comes from packaging of different sorts—paper, glass, metal and plastic. Packaging is important—it protects products and ensures hygiene—but a lot of packaging is simply there to catch our eye, to make us buy this rather than that. What we should be careful about is how much we use and how much we throw away.

One way to cut down on waste is to recycle wherever possible. That means putting bottles in bottle banks and finding somewhere to take old newspapers. Another way is to re-use. That means, for example, returning milk bottles to be cleaned and used again or, where possible, returning soft-drink bottles to the shop from which they came.

Glass
Glass is largely made from sand—and there's hardly a shortage of that in the world. However, the sand has to be dug up and this leaves unpleasant gashes in the landscape. More importantly, glass-making uses enormous amounts of energy. Much less energy—and much less sand—is used if old glass is recycled—melted down to be made into new bottles and jars.

Every tonne of crushed waste glass used saves the equivalent of 135 litres (30 gallons) of oil. So by taking used glass to your local bottle bank you really are helping the environment. Don't forget—you can take more than just bottles; empty jam jars will do as well, but remember to take the lids off first!

Paper
Britain uses the wood from more than *130 million* trees a year to make paper and cardboard for such things as newspapers, magazines, junk mail, kitchen towels, tissues and boxes. It takes a lot less time to use these things and chuck them out than it does to grow another 130 million trees, even if they are fast-growing softwoods such as pine. Britain only grows about 10 per cent of the trees it uses.

The manufacture of paper uses tremendous amounts of energy and can cause much pollution from poisonous wastes which kill wildlife when they find their way into rivers and seas (see page 24). And when land is cleared for plantations of trees, wildlife habitats are lost.

Believe it or not
Over *7 billion* drinks cans are thrown away in Britain every year. Placed end to end they would reach further than the Moon! Almost half of them are aluminium and could be recycled—but currently only 3 or 4 out of every hundred are!

Metals

Some tin cans are made partly of tin, but they also contain steel and, increasingly, aluminium. All these metals have to be mined from the ground and this can be damaging to the local landscape. Since the 1950s, manufacturers have made the tins thinner, using less material, and this has helped. But we could be doing much more, particularly by recycling the metals we use.

Aluminium is made from a mineral called bauxite. It takes four tonnes of bauxite to make *one* tonne of aluminiu Aluminium is used for making drink cans and for such things as milk bott tops, some takeaway and frozen foo containers, and the little cups use for instance, to hold some individu fruit pies. Also, of course, the foil which many cooks wrap around the turkey at Christmas.

Aluminium can be melted down and recycled again and again. This saves enormous amounts of energ and bauxite We should tr not to use to much aluminium, but when we do, recycling i is one of the ways we can bes help the environment. And yo can make some money doing it! (Se page 78.)

Believe it or not
Two days' issues of the *Sun* newspaper, with one paper piled on top of another would stretch higher than the top of Everest.

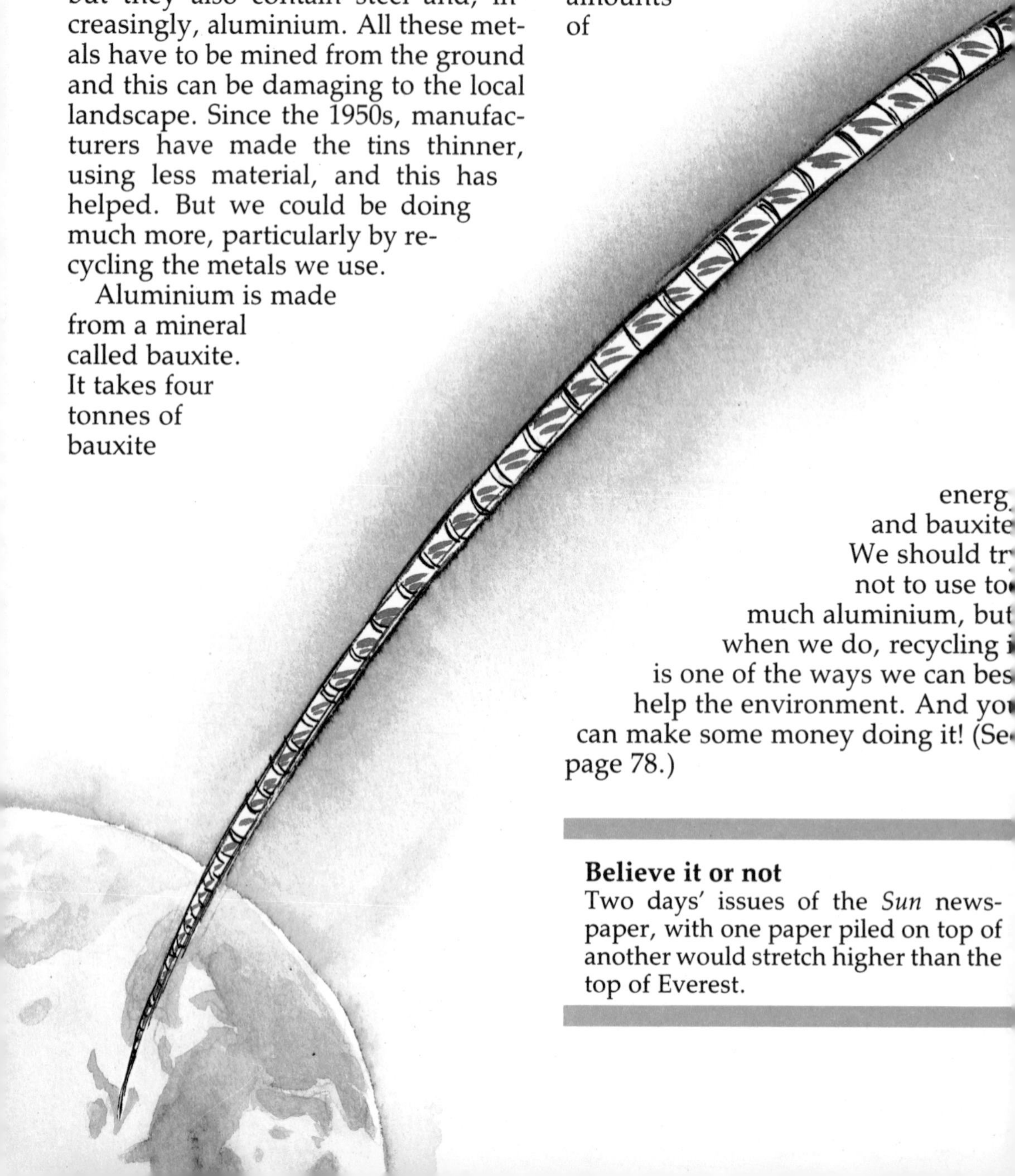

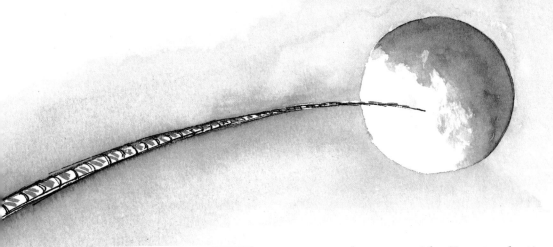

streets and countryside. Empty plastic bags and bottles can even be found in Antarctica and on the slopes of Mount Everest.

One of the problems with plastics is that they are not fully biodegradable. That means they don't rot and disappear completely. So food that we consume within minutes is wrapped in materials which last for hundreds of years!

You can now get plastic bags designed to break up slowly when they are thrown away but they do not yet disappear entirely.

Believe it or not
Every single day, Britain produces enough rubbish to fill Trafalgar Square—up to the top of Nelson's Column.

Plastics
Well over a third of the packaging we use is made from plastics. There are over 50 types, made from non-renewable materials such as oil, coal and natural gas. In Britain very little of this plastic is recycled. It goes into our dustbins and ends up in holes in the ground. The rest lies around in our

YGC Action

Watch out for over-packaging, e.g. small packets of crisps inside larger packets. Re-use plastic carrier bags. Better still, use a cloth bag. Recycle by collecting glass and paper products and aluminium cans and taking them to your nearest collection point.

The Bathroom

Having a bath? Washing your hair? Cleaning your teeth? You've probably realised by now that environmental issues affect every part of our lives. Here are some of the points to think about next time you're in the bathroom.

Baths and showers
Do you know that if you have a shower instead of a bath you use about half as much water and it doesn't need to be so hot? So you save both water *and* some of the energy used to heat it.

Now take a look at the bottles and pots on the bathroom shelf. You'll probably find bubblebath, talcum powder, skin cleanser, moisturisers and shampoos. Individually these may not cause much harm to the environment but many of us have a great selection of them. Imagine how much cardboard, plastic, glass and metal has been used to package them. Do you think your household might be able to make do with fewer and perhaps buy items which aren't so extravagantly packaged?

Deodorant, Hairspray and Shaving foam
We have already mentioned 'ozone friendly' aerosols (page 11), but ozone-friendly doesn't necessarily mean environment-friendly. For one thing, aerosols are very wasteful of

ackaging because only two-thirds of ɪe can contains the substance you're ɪsing. The rest is needed for the pro- ɪellant which forces the contents out ɪrough the nozzle. Another problem ɪ that, unlike some cans (see page 30), ɪerosols are not very suitable for re- ɪycling. The answer, if you use de- ɪdorants, is to use roll-ons (especially ɪnes you can refill) or trigger- and ɪump-action sprays.

ɪhe loo
ɪne-third of the total amount of water ɪsed in a household every day is used ɪ flush the loo! On page 24 you can

ɪnd out how much is needed for each ɪush and also how we can pollute the ɪater by using lavatory cleaners. Is ɪour bottle labelled to say that it does ɪot damage the environment? If so, it ɪ probably one of the brands which ɪoes not contain the strong bleaches ɪnd other chemicals that can pollute ɪe water when poured down the loo. ɪhese more 'environment-friendly' ɪrands are now sold by many super- ɪarkets and health-food shops.

Some people hang special loo cleaners in the bowl to colour and clean the water with every flush. We think these are unnecessary and they send more pollutants down the drain. Ask the adults in your house to put them on their list of things they could do without (see page 78).

Loo paper
The average family flushes away liter- ally *miles* of loo paper every year. You can find out how much your house- hold sends down the drain by multi- plying the length of each roll (it should be given on the outside of the packet) by the number of loo rolls you use each week. Multiply that number by 52 and you've got the total for the whole year. You'll be surprised by the amount. We know that using lots of paper is not good for our environment (see page 29) and that we should try to use less wherever possible. But at least it's not so bad if the paper has been recycled. Many shops now sell brands of soft loo roll made from recycled paper. Look on the packet to see whether yours is one of these. It's particularly good if the label says '100% recycled'.

You might also find that the packet says 'non-chlorine bleached'. Loo paper is bleached to make it bright white. Even coloured paper is bleached before it is dyed. But sometimes bleaching can produce poisonous chemicals called dioxins which, if they find their way from the factories into rivers, can kill fish and other wildlife. 'Non-chlorine bleaching' does not create this problem. There are also papers which are not bleached at all. They are an off-white colour which some people think looks grubby. But that shouldn't worry us if it's better for the fish.

Loo seats

Is your loo seat plastic or wooden? If it's wooden is it made from light or dark coloured wood? If it's dark it may be mahogany in which case it will almost definitely have come from a rainforest. It's too late to worry about it now, so don't stop using it! But if your family needs to buy a new loo seat in the future, encourage them *not* to choose one made from a tropical hardwood. Occasionally, there are loo seats for sale made from wood from a forest which is carefully looked after so that some trees can be cut down without destroying the whole area. If a loo seat is labelled to tell people this then it should be quite all right to buy it. It should be labelled, *wood from a sustainably managed forest.*

The medicine cabinet

Medicines help protect us against disease, and help us to get better once we are ill. But many are poisonous taken in the wrong way—or by the wrong people. Most medicines are now packaged in containers designed to stop very young children from opening them by mistake. But you also see a great deal of over packaging. Chemists often sell medicines in a bottle or tube, itself contained within a box. And then they put it in a paper bag. *Triple* packaging!

Also, remember that many medicines are based on plants which originally came from the rainforests. When we destroy the forests, we lessen the chance of finding other vital medicines.

Shampoos and Hair conditioners

While these do not cause serious water pollution, it is a good idea to use them sparingly. Watch out for double packaging—and, like soap, try to buy cruelty-free brands.

Shaving

You may not have to shave in the morning, but for those members of your family who do, remember the following points:

- Disposable plastic razors produce much more rubbish (the empty packet and the used razor are both thrown away) than razors you use again and again.

- Shaving foam packed in a tube is more 'environment-friendly' than that packed in an aerosol.

- Electric razors are actually more energy efficient than ordinary razors, even though ordinary razors don't run on electricity! How can this be? The answer is that more energy is used in making shaving foam, aerosol cans and disposable razors than is needed for making and regularly using an electric razor.

- Run an electric razor from the plug rather than use a battery (see page 52).

- Avoid shaving brushes made from badger hair.

Soap
The plant oils or animal fats used to make soap do not seriously pollute the water. However, the dyes and perfumes may take longer to biodegrade so it is better to use soaps that are colourless and unscented. Perhaps you sometimes buy soaps as a birthday or Christmas present. Look out for cruelty-free brands.

Toothpaste
Did you know that a chemical called titanium dioxide is used to make toothpaste white? It's not bad for you, but it's not so good for the environment, because it produces an unpleasant waste when the toothpaste is being made. Gel toothpastes do not use titanium dioxide.

The Kitchen

From eating breakfast, to washing up, to making a bedtime drink, there are dozens of ways in which you can be a Young Green Consumer in the kitchen. Here are a few of them.

Pass the parcel
If you've ever helped to unpack the shopping or noticed how quickly the waste bin fills up with empty boxes and bottles, you'll understand why the problem of wasteful packaging is important in the kitchen. Pages 28–31 tell you how rubbish can damage our environment.

Take a good look along the kitchen shelves. How many examples of overpackaging can you spot? Look for items wrapped in several layers. Are all those separate layers really necessary? Sometimes they are needed to keep food fresh or to prevent it being damaged. But not always. What about small packets of crisps within a larger bag? Or those ready-made meals which come in a tin-foil container, held in a cardboard 'sleeve' and wrapped in clear plastic film? Sometimes, so many layers have been peeled away that it looks as though there's been a game of pass the parcel.

Buying in bulk

Can you find anything in the cupboards packed in a giant-sized container—breakfast cereal, for example, or those big bottles of squash? Supermarkets sell numerous giant-size items, and if you've gone there in the car it's easy to get them back home. Shopping in this way is called 'buying in bulk' and it saves on packaging. A large packet of washing powder may contain three or four times as much as a small packet but the large box does not weigh three or four times as much as the small one.

However, using a large supermarket instead of your local shops is not always a good idea. Going there by car adds to pollution and traffic jams. So if only one or two things are needed and you have shops nearby, offer to walk or cycle to get them instead of someone hopping in the car.

Bags of waste

Do heaps of plastic bags fall out of the cupboard every time you open it? If so, someone in your family is probably bringing home a new carrier bag every time they go to the shops. Is it you? Take a used one with you next time and you won't be adding to the mountains of non-biodegradable plastic on the rubbish tips.

Better still, use a proper shopping bag or basket which lasts for years. If you are still left with some old carrier bags, they can be used to line the pedal bin instead of new plastic bin liners.

Buying organic

Since more and more shoppers ar worried that the chemicals spread o the soil or sprayed on crops can caus pollution (see page 22) and may not b good for our health, supermarket have begun to join the health foo shops in selling organic food.

Fruit and vegetables are the mo: common form of organic food foun on sale. But there are other things tha have been made from the crops— cereal and bread and jam, for instance There are also foods produced by an mals or insects which feed o the chemical-free plants—milk an honey are two. Animals fed in thi way are also free of hormones an antibiotics fed to intensively farme beasts.

At the moment, organic food i often more expensive than foo grown using chemicals because:

- Organic farming is more labou: intensive and so wage bills ar higher.

- In the course of a year, fewer crop can be grown on an organic far: than on the same area of lan farmed with chemicals.

- Since there are still very few o: ganic farms, they produce smaller range of food and the cannot guarantee a regular suppl to the shops. This means th farmers' profits are likely to b lower and, because they cann deliver in bulk, their transpo: costs are higher.

- Supermarkets insist on packagin organic fruit and vegetable: adding to the cost, so that they d not become mixed up with nor organic food.

37

So don't be surprised if the shoppers in your family won't always buy organic. But if they do so only sometimes, or make it clear to the shopkeepers that they would if the prices were lower, then your household is helping to ensure that more organic food is grown and sold and fewer chemicals are used on the land.

GREEN GRUB

Breakfast cereals
Most of us love those small variety packs, but next time you ask for them, remember how much cardboard and plastic is used to make them. Larger boxes are less wasteful.

Did you know that if you like muesli in the mornings, and you find pieces of brazil nuts in your bowl, you'll be eating a rainforest-friendly breakfast! (See page 40.)

And if you want to try organically grown cereals, it is possible to buy them in supermarkets as well as in health food shops.

Milk
Open your fridge. Is the milk in a glass bottle, a plastic bottle or a carton? The best thing is to have it in a glass bottle—but *only* if the bottle goes back to the milkman or the shop. It can then be used again and again (up to 50 times) instead of being thrown away as soon as it's empty. So if the milk-

man delivers bottles, it's a good idea t buy from him (or her) rather than buy ing cartons or plastic bottles from th shops. Since almost 20 million litres o milk are drunk in Britain every day you can really cut down on you rubbish by switching to glass mi bottles.

Cream
Is there any cream in the fridge? If s is it in small, individual servings, or a aerosol can rather than the more com mon plastic pots? Both the individu servings and the aerosols waste pack aging and aerosols are particularly di ficult to recycle. What's more, you g less cream than you imagine in the ca because so much space is taken up b the propellant (see page 32).

Butter and Cheese
Try not to use individually wrappe portions at home or in restauran and be on the look out for 'organi varieties.

Eggs
Next time you fry an egg, look at th colour of the yolk. The British prefer deep, rich yellow yolk but this is n always its natural colour and is ofte produced by adding dyes to the hen food. The dark colour doesn't mea as many people suppose, that the eg is healthier or tastier. Eggs from her which have been fed organically wit out colouring and added chemica may have paler yolks but they tas just as good.

'Free-range' eggs are not necessari organic and so the yolks may still b dark, but at least the hens have n been factory farmed (see page 23 Which would you prefer? To be stu in a small cage with four other bir that spend most of their time peckin at you or out in the open as a fre

ange hen pecking in the ground for ood? Look out for the free-ange eggs which are now sold in many shops.

Look, too, at the box the eggs are acked in. Is it foam plastic, clear plas-c or cardboard (paper pulp)? The manufacturers of plastic egg boxes say nat less energy is used to make them nan is used to make cardboard boxes. ut we still think the paper pulp ones re better. Not only are they made om recycled paper but they bio-egrade when finally thrown away. Vhichever type of box your eggs come n, try to re-use it as many times as ossible. While supermarkets don't llow you to take back your old egg oxes for refilling, many small shops o. Another point in favour of paper ulp boxes is that they often last onger than boxes made from foam lastic, which tend to break up more uickly.

lour and Bread

Many people believe that wholemeal r wholewheat flour (which contains ll the wheat grain, with nothing dded or taken away) is best for us, ut perhaps the best thing for our nvironment is if the grain is grown rganically. It is possible to buy or-anic flours and bread and if you have sweet tooth, see if you can find rganic cakes!

Fruit and Vegetables

Eating organic

Nowadays, you can find organic fruit and vegetables in most large super-markets as well as in farm and health food shops. But some people don't like it because:

- they think it doesn't look so appetising
- it's usually more expensive.

Firstly, it depends on what you mean by appetising. Carrots grown without chemicals, for example, come in all shapes and sizes. There's nothing wrong with that. They might also have holes where pests have nibbled them, but they are just as tasty and some people say they are even better.

As for price, it's true that organic fruit and vegetables tend to be more expensive (see page 36) so don't be surprised if you can't always persuade your family to buy them. But the more people who choose them, even occa-sionally, the cheaper they will be-come.

Peel or pack

Nature often makes the best packag-ing. Think of orange peel and nut-shells . . . So do we really need plastic nets around our oranges, onions

or brussels sprouts? And why buy potatoes in a plastic bag when you can buy them loose and take them home loose in your shopping basket?

You may be particularly annoyed to come across organic fruit and vegetables which are packaged in plastic. This is often the case in supermarkets where the staff say they don't want the organic foods to be muddled up with the rest.

Strawberries in winter?

We have become very used to eating summer food such as lettuces, cucumbers, tomatoes and strawberries throughout the year. Also to having our pick of exotic fruit and vegetables from distant countries—mangoes, lychees, avocados, aubergines, peppers are just some. But be aware that a great deal of energy is used either to heat greenhouses (for lettuces and cucumbers, for instance) or to transport the food long distances by plane, ship or lorry. So by not insisting on strawberries and cream in the depths of winter, you are doing your bit for energy efficiency.

Honey

Bees produce honey by collecting pollen and nectar from plants and it may be that these plants have been sprayed with pesticides. Some people would rather have 'organic' honey (the plants haven't been sprayed with chemicals) but the beekeepers stress that although the bees are encouraged

to fly towards organically grown plants, there is no guarantee that they will end up there!

Ice-cream and Yoghurt

Most of us love ice-cream but next time you choose some, think about the packaging. A big tub is obviously better than several small ones! You might also like to see whether your ice-cream is made with natural flavourings, such as real fruit, rather than with chemical flavourings. The same is true of yoghurt. Take a look on the tub and see what the label says.

Some healthfood shops sell organic yoghurt and ice-creams.

Nuts

Have you heard of Chico Mendes? He campaigned for reserves in the Brazilian rainforest. The trees in the reserves would be protected from fell

g and burning so that local people uld earn their living by harvesting, r example, rubber and brazil nuts. hico Mendes was murdered by his nemies in 1988, but his supporters ntinue to campaign for the reserves.

So you can help the survival of the inforests by eating *brazil nuts*. The ore you eat, the more the Brazilians ll, the more money they earn and e less likely they are to destroy the inforests. Since brazil nuts only ow in rainforests, you can be sure hen you are eating one that you are eing a green consumer and helping save trees.

ooking oil

hat sort of cooking oil is used at ome? Sunflower, safflower, corn, live oil perhaps? Or does the bottle st say 'Vegetable Oil'? If so, it may ntain rape seed oil from the crop hich is fast turning our countryside ellow. You have probably noticed the rilliantly coloured fields but, al- ough you may like them, they create ome problems. The plant has only ecently been introduced to this coun- y and has brought with it new pests hich have no natural predators. lso, doctors believe the pollen may ause hay fever.

ish

ow many fish fingers do you eat in a ear? 50, 100, 500, 5,000. . . ? And do ou eat fish burgers and fish and chips o? Fish is a healthy and very popular food. So popular that the number of fish in the seas has dropped alarm- ingly. Too many are being caught— often more than are wanted. Some large fishing vessels suck fish out of the water just like a vacuum cleaner sucks up dust. The trouble with this is that the fishermen can't choose what they catch. Along with the fish they're *allowed* to catch, they are killing thou- sands of others, including young fish which cannot be replaced.

One way to provide more fish with- out stripping the oceans is to breed them in fish farms. Most of our salmon and trout are bred on farms. But there are still problems.

- The waste produced by the farms can cause water pollution.

- The farmed fish may breed new diseases and if they escape they can infect wild fish.

- Fish-eating birds and animals such as herons and seals are killed be- cause fish farmers want to protect their stock.

There's very little you can do about the problems of fish-farming. But there is another fishy problem about which you *can* do something. That is the kill- ing of dolphins by some tuna fisher- men. Schools of dolphins often swim with the tuna and if the fishermen are using nets the dolphins will be caught as well. Of no use to the fishermen,

they will be thrown back in the water, dead or seriously injured. Fortunately, not all tuna are caught by net—some are caught on a long fishing line. So there is less danger to dolphins. The varieties likely to have been caught on a line are: skipjack, albacore, bonito and white meat tuna. Yellowfin tuna is more likely to have been caught by net.

To help save the dolphins check the label on your next tin of tuna to see which variety it contains and look out for brands which state that their fish have been caught on a line.

Chicken and Turkeys

Each week in Britain, about 9 million poultry birds are killed. Most of them will have been farmed intensively, in crowded conditions with little or no access to daylight. If you are a green consumer who eats chicken and turkey, ask for 'free-range' birds.

Meat

Not everybody eats meat. About three per cent of British adults are vegetarian while about one in ten children are said by their parents to be either completely vegetarian or beginning to avoid red meat such as beef, pork and lamb. Everyone who *is* a meat eater should know that it is possible to buy meat which comes from animals reared in more pleasant conditions than are found on intensive farms. This method also saves on pollution (see page 23). In addition, the meat contains no colouring, preservatives or chemical additives. This meat is often called 'Real Meat'.

DRINKS ALL ROUND!

How many different things do you drink each day? A glass of water? mug of tea? A carton of fruit juice or canned fizzy drink? There is a much wider variety of drinks on sale than there used to be and we buy many more of them. That means we throw much more away—empty cans and cartons, used teabags, for example. Here are some of the things you should know about what you drink:

Fizzy drinks and Fruit juices

The average person in Britain consumes over 60 litres of fizzy drink every year. In America the figure is 163 litres each! The waste from the packaging is tremendous although it varies depending on the type of container:

- *Individual cartons* may be convenient, but for one small drink you throw away the carton, a plastic straw and its plastic wrapping.

- *Drink cans* are often made of aluminium. Look for the *alu* sign or test the side of the can with a magnet (if it doesn't stick, the can is aluminium). Flip through to page 78 to see how these cans may be recycled. Remember not to throw ring-pulls

away (or on the ground). They too can be sent for recycling.

- *Glass bottles* can be collected and taken to the bottle bank. Don't forget to keep the metal lids for the can bank, if there is one.

- *Plastic bottles* are often used for fizzy drinks and squashes. Many are made from a plastic called PET (polyethylene terephthalate) which is suitable for recycling. Unfortunately, however, there are very few places you can take empty PET bottles at the moment. But get to know which plastics are which so that you'll be ready for the day you *can* recycle them. Some supermarkets now tell you on the label if the bottle is made of PET. Have a look next time you go shopping.

o which type of packaging should the reen consumer choose? It's difficult o say, but *as long as you recycle the bottle* hen glass is probably the best at the moment.

Britons guzzle around a billion litres f fruit juice and fruit drinks every ear. That's nearly three million litres very day! Fruit juice may be good for our health, but it's not always so ood for our environment. Fruit rmers grow only a few different spees and have to protect them with erbicides and insecticides. We also now that rainforest areas have been nder threat from fruit juice comanies wanting to use the land for fruit lantations.

Also, as with fizzy drinks, think bout the packaging your juice comes . Can it be recycled? You may feel at you won't accept any drink that is ackaged in materials that can't yet be ecycled.

Tea, Coffee and Cocoa

Most of us enjoy a cup of tea—in fact, 70 billion cups of tea are drunk in Britain every year! Usually tea has no artificial colourings or preservatives and, unless milk or sugar are added, is calorie-free. Recently, some shops have started to sell organic teas.

But next time you fling a teabag into a mug, think about the paper wasted. You can get special spoons, which are like a cross between a sieve and a pair of scissors. You put a spoonful of tea leaves into them, then pour on boiling water. They can be used again and again (changing the tea leaves each time, of course!). Another point with teabags—the bags are made from

bleached fibres. Some manufacturers are now planning to switch to un-bleached materials, so keep a look out for these in the shops. You can already get unbleached filter papers for coffee machines.

One thing you should know about tea, coffee and also about cocoa is that the crops from which they come are mostly grown on land that was once rainforest. This does not mean they *cause* rainforest destruction—usually the crops are planted after the trees have been cleared for other purposes. But the fact that money can be made from these plantations once the rain-forest has disappeared means there are further incentives for the trees to be destroyed rather than protected.

Bottled water

There has been a boom in demand for bottled water. Just count the varieties on the shelves next time you go to the supermarket. People sometimes don't like the taste of tap water, or they are suspicious that it may not be very healthy. Yet, in general, tap water is perfectly safe to drink, and no plastic or glass bottles have been used in get-ting it to you. You may be interested to know that bottled waters cost around 600 times more than tap water!

Some people believe they are being 'green' by using a water filter but it's much more 'green' to campaign for clean tap water. If your family has a water filter jug, however, make sure the instructions are followed carefully.

Wine, Beer and Spirits

If these are drunk in your home, are the glass bottles saved for the bottle bank? Test the cans to see whether they are aluminium. And does any-one in the household know you can buy organic wines, champagnes and beers?

44

FAST FOOD AND TAKEAWAYS

Most of us like to eat pizzas, burgers, fish and chips or Chinese takeaway sometimes. But on your next visit to a fast-food restaurant, take a look at the piles of empty cartons waiting for your food. If you're taking the meal home they keep it warm, but what's the point if you're eating in the restaur-ant? Time how long it is from the moment you're given your food to the moment you throw away the carton. Not long, is it. Did you really need it in the first place? In some restaurants the food is wrapped in paper instead, so at least the rubbish is less bulky.

It's not only the cartons that are thrown away either, but fistfuls of pa-per napkins, cups and plastic straws, together with individual packets of

ketchup and mayonnaise, salt and pepper. Some of them have not even been used.

Most fast-food restaurants create all this waste because their meals are de-signed for speed and convenience.

he more we ask for food served up in seconds, the more waste we're likely to cause. The same is true of takeaway meals you eat at home. Although you may be using your own plates and cutlery, the food comes to you in a throwaway carton—usually aluminium—instead of in a saucepan or serving dish which can be washed and used again. And try to avoid paper plates and plastic cutlery at home too, even if it means you have to do the washing up.

So if you're a fast-food freak, or even if you enjoy it just occasionally, try not to take so many of the disposable bits and pieces that come with it. And choose those restaurants which you think cause less waste than others. You could ask the manager of the restaurant whether they recycle any of their rubbish and whether they use recycled paper.

And don't forget to put your litter in the bin. The empty bags and cartons blowing around our streets are one of the most annoying forms of urban pollution.

Many green consumers have wor-

ried for a long time that plastic foam-blown burger cartons are made with CFCs. You'll be pleased to know, however, that many chains in Britain no longer use CFCs.

Another concern has been that hamburger chains might use beef from cattle raised on ranches created by felling and burning rainforests. But some chains are now making sure the beef they use does not come from areas in which tropical rainforest has recently been cleared.

As long as so many people all over the world eat fast-food burgers more and more beef will be needed and the tropical rainforests will continue to suffer.

SWEETS

If you've got a sweet tooth, you'll be glad to know that sweets are not seen as the No. 1 threat to the environment. But here are one or two things to think about next time you unwrap a tasty gum or tip out some chocolate raisins.

Most sweets are loaded with sugar, which we all know is dangerous for your teeth and gums. But what about the dangers for the environment?

Sugar comes either from sugar cane or sugar beet. Cane comes from tropical countries, beet from Europe. Both may be treated with various chemicals and there are other problems too. In Australia, for example, the sugar cane plantations have sometimes helped to cause soil erosion, which is blanketing areas of the Great Barrier Reef with mud and silt. As a result, reef creatures are suffocated. And have you seen the car ads on British TV which feature burning sugar cane fields? They are burnt off after the harvest just as stubble is burnt in other countries. Enormous amounts of smoke and carbon dioxide are produced and wildlife is destroyed. Another problem is that the refineries which make sugar from beet or cane can cause serious pollution. One company in Britain accidentally spilled a large quantity of sugar syrup into a nearby river—and killed thousands of fish.

The most important thing to watch out for with sweets, however, is over-packaging. Millions of sweets are sold every day and that means millions of wrappers are thrown away. Just think of this: if all the Kit-Kat bars sold around the world every *hour* were stacked flat, one on top of another, they would make a pile over 2 km high. That is five times the height of the Empire State Building! And each bar comes with two layers of wrapping, one paper and one silver foil. How much of that ends up on the streets? Remember never to drop sweet wrappers as you're walking along. In some parts of the country the pavements and gutters are so full of them you can hardly see the ground!

So here are some pointers for the sweet-toothed:

- Avoid over-packaged sweets, particularly multi-packs or mini-bars, and ask the shopkeeper not to put your already wrapped sweets in a bag—even a paper bag.

- If you're buying sweets anyway, look out for the brands which tell you that some of the money you pay goes to support wildlife.

- Cut down on the number of sweets you eat and you could be treating yourself to better health in a few years' time.

- Decide whether sweets could sometimes go on your 'What could I do without?' list (see page 78).

UNDER THE SINK

When was the last time you had t clean the bath, polish the front doc knob or wash the dishes? A great dea of cleaning goes on in most house holds. In fact, add up all the time spen washing, hoovering and polishing i the average British home and i amounts to 31 days a year! That mean that for many of us the cupboard un der the sink is full of bottles, tins an boxes of liquid cleaners, polishes an detergents. It's a strange fact, but al this effort to clean the house can caus pollution elsewhere.

Washing powder
Take a look at the box. Does it claim t be a 'green' powder, perhaps labelled 'environment-friendly' or 'phosphate

ree'? Public concern about problems washing powders can cause when they drain into rivers and streams has ed some brands to alter their ingredients. One of the major changes has been to leave out the chemicals called phosphates. These help with the cleaning and also help to produce suds, but in lakes and some rivers they can cause algae to grow so fast that all the oxygen is used up and other life forms suffocate. (Washing powders are not the only source of phosphates. They are also contained in human sewage and often in the chemicals which drain off farm land (see page 23 and page 25).)

Whatever brand is bought in your household it is best to use as little as possible since washing powders are concentrated chemicals. Most ordinary powders include *surfactants* which do most of the cleaning; *bleach* to remove stains and to stop white clothes going yellow; *brighteners and whiteners* to make the clean washing look even brighter; and *preservatives* to stop the powder going mouldy. One concern about surfactants, for instance, is that they are based on petroleum. Petroleum is a non-renewable resource and the industry can cause great damage to the environment through oil spills.

If you see the word 'biological' on the pack, don't confuse it with 'biodegradable' (an environmental buzzword which, for detergents, means that the ingredients break down and stop working in the waste system). 'Biological' means that the powder contains *enzymes* which help to dissolve stains and to make the powder work in cooler water.

To say that a powder is 'green' can mean a variety of things. Some brands have just replaced the phosphates while others have changed most of the ingredients. It may be difficult to tell how much less polluting 'green' powders are than ordinary brands but it is still worth buying them since they are forcing the makers of all washing powders to look for ingredients which are kinder to the environment.

Nowadays, some manufacturers have begun to put a great deal of information about their ingredients and the environment on their boxes. Have a closer look at yours. You may be surprised by what you learn.

Bleach
Bleach is a strong chemical used to kill germs in sinks, loos and drains. Use it sparingly in order to cut down on water pollution. There are 'environment-friendly' cleaners on sale nowadays for most of the jobs traditionally tackled with bleach.

If you live in the country and have a septic tank instead of a link to the main drainage system you shouldn't use bleach at all. It kills the useful bacteria which break down the sewage so that it decomposes.

Washing-up liquid
Washing-up liquids have never contained phosphates, although some bottles are marked 'phosphate-free' to make you think they are less polluting than competitive brands. Washing-up

liquids do contain colourings and per-fumes, though, and most of the chem-icals which get rid of grease come from petroleum products.

Surface cleaners

These are used for sinks and worktops and contain only small amounts of phosphates but there are phosphate-free brands available which, like 'green' washing powders, use non-petroleum surfactants and are not usually tested on animals.

Polish

By using beeswax polish you are sup-porting beekeepers, helping to ensure that there are plenty of bees around. While you may not like their sting, they are very important to the coun-tryside. And beekeepers are often keen to see fewer pesticides used since the chemicals kill their bees.

If your cupboard is full of spray polishes then remember the problems of disposing of them (see page 33). Some polishes come in glass jars so you can take the empties to the bottle bank.

Oven cleaners

Many contain very strong chemicals but you can use a paste of baking soda (sodium bicarbonate) mixed with water instead.

Window cleaners

These are not a major problem but we think it better to use a trigger pack than an aerosol can.

48

FOIL AND FILM

Aluminium foil

You have probably used aluminium foil, if not for cooking then for dress-ing up or for Christmas decorations. The aluminium is made from a mineral called bauxite which is found mainly in tropical countries where its mining may destroy areas of rainforest. Energy is used in transporting the bauxite long distances from the mines to factories in other countries, includ-ing Britain. It also takes a great deal of energy to turn the bauxite into alumin-ium. As with aluminium cans, foil can be recycled (see page 78) and this takes only a fifth of the energy used to make it from scratch. Better still, try to do without foil altogether.

Clingfilm

This soft, clingy, see-through wrap-ping is easy to use but people often use too much when they could make do with a reusable container such as a tupperware box.

Plastic washing bowls and buckets

At the moment, we can't buy things made from recycled plastic but if we complain long and loud enough to the manufacturers we may be able to help persuade them to use it.

Another thing you should know is that a poisonous metal called cad-mium is sometimes used in making bright orange, red or yellow plastics. You will not be poisoned by the cad-mium in plasticware but if there is an accident in the factory that makes it then the cadmium can pollute the area round about. Better that manufac-turers don't use it at all.

Saucepan handles

Watch out for wooden handles made from tropical hardwoods.

MACHINES EAT ENERGY

The machines in your kitchen will nearly all run on electricity. Any machine that gives out heat (like a cooker) or heats something else (the water in a washing machine, a dishwasher or a kettle), or has a moving part (a tumble drier or a washing machine), uses much more electricity than a light, radio or a television. So we should be particularly careful not to use them wastefully. Large amounts of energy are also used in the factories which made the machines so we should try to make our fridges, cookers or washing machines last for as long as possible. When your family is buying a new one, you should try to find out from the manual how much energy (and water for a washing machine or dishwasher) the machine uses. The information is usually there if you look hard enough. Another important thing is to buy a machine which is the right size for your family's needs.

Cookers

Gas cookers are more energy-efficient than electric cookers and they cause less carbon dioxide pollution. But, whether your family has a gas or an electric cooker, there are several ways to make cooking more energy-efficient:

- Using a double steamer or pressure cooker.

- Not heating the oven just for one bread roll.

- Putting several things in the oven at once. If your cooker has both a small and a large oven, use the smaller one whenever you can.

- Keeping lids on saucepans if possible, especially to heat liquid. It will boil faster with a lid on.

- Not overcooking vegetables!

Fridges and Freezers

Fridges contain CFCs (see page 10). But you need not worry—the CFCs don't stream out every time you open the fridge door! They are only released

when the fridge is thrown out and it is now usually possible to find a dump that disposes of the old fridge safely and recycles the CFCs.

One thing you can do every day, though, is to make sure you close the fridge door properly. If it is left open, the fridge uses more energy in trying to keep cool. Fridges and freezers use more energy when they're empty than when they're full. If you can't fill the freezer, packing it with screwed up newspaper will help.

Kettles

Take a look inside your kettle and you'll probably find that the tubes or elements are covered in a hard 'fur'.

This is because much of the water we use is 'hard' water. It contains calcium, which clings to metal and causes the fur. This makes the kettle work less efficiently, therefore using more electricity. (If you live in an area with soft water you won't have the same problem.)

There are products to de-fur kettles—and shower heads, which can also be affected in this way. A strong solution of vinegar in water works just as well.

And if you're trying to help reduce acid rain and the Greenhouse Effect, use the water in the kettle as soon as it's boiled. Don't go away and forget it and then have to switch on the kettle again when you come back.

Washing machines

Next time you throw your dirty clothes into the washing machine,

stop and think a minute. While it' washing them, the machine will cor sume:

- energy
- water

If the machine is not being properl used it might be wasting larg amounts of both. In order to b energy-efficient and water-efficient i is better:

- To put a full load in the machin for every wash.

- If there is not enough for a ful load, to make sure the econom setting is on, if there is one.

- To make sure the temperature o the water is not too high—runnin; the machine on the correct pro gramme for the type of materia being washed.

Remember, also, it is wasteful to us too much washing powder.

Tumble driers

These guzzle energy in order to turr the drum inside and to heat the air. I your household has a tumble drier don't use it just for the odd piece o clothing, like swimming trunks or costume, which can easily be driec outside or on the end of a radiator Also, it is not good to leave the ma chine rumbling away long after th clothes are dry. Better to test then from time to time and only leave ir those that are still damp. In America new machines have been developec which switch off automatically wher the clothes are dry.

Dishwashers

If your household has a dishwasher follow the same dos and don't suggested for the use of washing machines.

The Sitting Room

Picture this. A family is sitting around a gas fire, watching the TV. A dog is stretched out on the carpet. In the background, rows of shelves groan with books, records and ornaments.

Now let's look at the scene from a slightly different angle. The TV may well be showing a programme or a video about the environment—there are plenty about these days. But your own sitting room might be helping to cause some of the problems that are flickering across the screen.

Fire

Every time we burn gas, coal, oil or logs we send carbon dioxide into the atmosphere and make it more likely that the Greenhouse Effect will change our weather. So, unless there's an old person or a small baby in the room, burn just enough to keep warm without getting boiling hot.

If you are starting a fire and plan to use firelighters, stop a moment. Fire-lighters are made from oil, which is non-renewable, and can cause pollu-tion. You can use dried strips of orange peel instead—and they smell nicer!

If your house has central heating, ask whether there is a room ther-mostat. There should be. This switches the system off when a certain temperature is reached. And it switches on again if the house cools down too much. If you do have a thermostat,

- where is it?

- what is the temperature setting?

20°C (68°F) is usually comfortable for a living room, but if your thermostat is located in a cool place, the boiler will keep on roaring until *that* place has reached 20°C. The sitting room, mean-while, will have been getting hotter and hotter.

Furniture

Check to see whether any of the furni-ture, including shelves, is made from tropical hardwoods, taken from the rainforests. If you do find some, don't

worry *too* much. There's nothing you can do about it now, but suggest to your family that if they are buying new furniture they avoid tropical hardwood unless it is labelled *wood from a sustainably managed forest*.

Windows

Look to see if the windows in the sitting room—and in any other parts of the house—are double-glazed. Heat escapes easily through glass, and double-glazing (two layers of glass with air in between) helps to keep warmth in the house. This is because the heat cannot pass as easily through the layer of air as it can through the glass. If you *don't* have double-glazing, don't expect things to change overnight just because you tell your family it is better for the environment. Double-glazing is expensive to install, but in the end saves money by cutting down the heating bills. Filling any gaps between the window and the

frame with strips of newspapers o cloth will stop draughts in winter an drawing curtains at night will help t keep the heat in.

Batteries

How many pieces of equipment ru off batteries in your house? Radios cassette players, clocks, electroni toys? Start a list and you might b surprised how many batteries yo use. In Britain we get through a total c 400 million a year! Unfortunately, ba teries are an environmental hazard They take up to 50 times more energ to make than they ever provide an they contain poisonous materials such as mercury and cadmium, whic cause pollution when the batteries ar thrown away.

So whenever you can, use main electricity instead. When you do hav to use batteries, look out for pack of 'green' batteries which state tha the batteries have a reduced o

zero mercury or cadmium content.

Even better, use rechargeable batteries. They are more expensive to buy in the first place (and you will need a recharger) but since you can recharge them at least 1,000 times they are cheaper in the long run. One problem with them is that they all contain high levels of cadmium. A scheme has been set up to recycle some brands of rechargeable batteries so if you do use them, check on the packet to see where you can send them for recycling.

Music

Apart from running cassette players and radios from the mains rather than from batteries whenever you can, remember not to keep them running when you leave the room. It's particularly important with cassettes (and record players) since they include a motor to turn the tape or disc. This means that they need more electricity than, for example, a radio.

We have not uncovered any major problems with records, cassettes or compact discs. If you can think of any, write and let us know! But record companies could try to make the record sleeves out of recycled paper. And what about tape boxes? They are always falling apart and are a waste of plastic. Someone should design a better box. Perhaps you should try . . .

Finally, most of us forget that our music can easily become someone else's pollution—noise pollution. If you like to listen to loud music think about wearing headphones, or playing it where no one else can hear you—either inside or outside the house. But be very careful not to have the volume too high even then. Listening to non-stop loud music can badly damage your hearing.

The Bedroom

While there are a number of the same things to investigate in the bedroom as in the sitting room—furniture, heating, batteries—there are others too. We've picked just a few:

Clothes

You can easily tell the difference between wool and cotton—both of which are natural materials since one comes from an animal and the other from a plant. But how good are you at distinguishing between natural and synthetic (man-made) fabrics? These include polyester, acrylic, rayon and nylon. The labels of your clothes should tell you from which materials they have been made but it is difficult to say whether one is definitely a better choice for green consumers than another since there are *some* problems with all of them. None is entirely 'environment friendly'. As a general rule, though, we recommend natural rather than synthetic fibres, all of which are made from oil.

Wool

Most of the wool we use comes from sheep, although it is also collected

from llamas and goats. Sheep, of course, are renewable and they don't need to be killed for their wool. The real issues to think about are sheep-dipping and the dyeing of wool. To control maggots and other pests that burrow into the sheep, farmers dip their animals in strong solutions of insecticide. These are very poisonous and can damage the environment if they are spilled into ponds or rivers.

Despite the possible pollution, however, wool is one of the 'greener' materials. It can also be recycled. If the second-hand shop fails to sell your old wool jersey, it can be sent off for recycling into tweed for skirts, jackets, hats and things.

Cotton
Much of the cotton from which our curtains, sheets and clothes are made is grown in the poorer countries of the world, and in order to produce as much as possible the farmers have become dependent on chemical fertilizers and pesticides. Cotton is a particularly greedy plant, quickly soaking up the nutrients (and water) from the earth, and if it is grown on the same piece of land for any length of time the soil may turn to dust and become useless for the cultivation of any crops at all.

You should also know that many fabrics, including most cotton, are bleached and dyed before they reach you and that this can cause pollution. It is now possible to buy unbleached and undyed cloth—but the cotton is not yet grown without chemicals.

Fur
Although much fur now comes from farmed animals, there have been strong protests about other creatures being caught in traps, particularly by Eskimos in Canada. We must not for-

get, though, that Eskimos depend for their living on the sale of furs. So to stop the trapping altogether would not be simple—nor fair to the Eskimos. But some of the trapping methods used are very cruel and it is important to make sure that any animal killed for our use is killed humanely. Also, of course, that it is not from any endangered species.

Even farmed animals create problems. Mink are vicious creatures and when they escape from the farms they cause havoc with birds and other wildlife. In many areas, they have driven otters—already an endangered species—from their old haunts.

Fake fur is now widely available and can look as good as the real thing. But it is made from oil-based synthetic fibres and therefore from non-renewable resources. Many people feel it is better to avoid these fabrics—and any fabric which imitates animal skin and fur—altogether.

Synthetic fibres
Although these are made from oil, they do have *some* advantages. One is that they are often easier to iron, which saves on electricity.

Green fashion
When green consumers start to ask in shops about how their clothes are made, fashion companies will have to

54

hink about environmental issues too. When they know that we want the materials which are doing the least harm to the planet they will have to provide them for us. So don't be afraid of talking about what you have earned and trying to find out more.

You might also like to try dressing in a 'green' style. One way is to wear T-shirts emblazoned with a 'green' message. There are plenty to choose from. And don't just throw clothes in the dustbin when they've gone out of fashion or you have outgrown them. It is a real waste of materials and the energy it took to make them. Keep them and you may find:

- They come back into fashion.

- You can wear them a different way—a large scarf could become a skirt.

- You can give them away to a charity shop or a jumble sale.

- Young children want to use them for dressing up.

- They can be torn up and used as cloths. This saves on the disposable cloths and paper towels often used in bathrooms and kitchens.

Jewellery

Many girls and women love jewellery, and so do plenty of men, but some of it is made from endangered animals. Ivory bracelets and necklaces are an obvious example but we often forget other things such as real tortoiseshell hair combs. Tortoises and turtles are now threatened species in many parts of the world. And if you or someone in your family has a coral necklace or earrings the coral will have come from a reef. Coral reefs are beautiful and very important parts of the underwater world, home to millions of plants and creatures. But they are beginning to disappear, partly because they are being polluted, partly because they are being blown up by people who use coral (like rock) for building, but partly also to feed our appetite for ornaments and jewellery. Avoid coral if you possibly can.

Diamonds

The mining and processing of diamonds requires enormous quantities of water. In some areas of the world this means draining swamps, which results in the destruction of the teeming wildlife that the swamps support.

The Okavango in Botswana is an unfortunate example of this problem. This is one of the most varied and beautiful marshland areas in the world, but it is threatened by development, including a highly productive diamond mine.

Gold

Gold mining has always caused considerable environmental damage whether the miners were cutting down trees to prop up the mine shafts, burning coal to free the gold from the ore, or using cyanide and mercury to process the gold. Cyanide and mercury have been particularly damaging where, as often happens, they found their way into rivers.

Many gold mines have been opened up in rainforest areas. In fact they have been responsible for a good deal of tropical deforestation. Not only is there the question of the mine itself and its spoil heaps, but also of the

housing for the workers and the transport links for moving the ore and gold to market. Once new roads are built, other people often use them to move into areas that were previously untouched.

Pearls

Pearls, as we all know, come from oysters. They are either harvested from wild oysters or cultured—which means putting a grain of sand or some other material inside an oyster, which then covers it with mother-of-pearl.

There is no major problem for the environment here, although it would be interesting to know whether pearl farmers have to pump chemicals into the sea to protect their oysters against parasites.

Shells

Collecting shells may be fun but the shell collector can also—knowingly or not—be an environmental vandal.

Picking up empty shells from the beach is fine. They are dead. But in many parts of the world there is now an industry which involves 'hoovering' the sea-bed of living shellfish.

Avoid both exotic shells and any trinkets made from them. And stay completely clear of shell shops.

Watches

Watches come in more shapes, sizes and colours than ever before and they are much cheaper than they used to be. They can be great fun but don't fall into the trap of collecting disposable watches which are thrown away the moment they stop ticking. They are a waste of plastic, metal and packaging.

If your watch uses button cell batteries ask at the shop what they do with the old ones. Batteries are polluting if thrown away but some shops have them collected for recycling. Better still, wear a solar-powered watch.

Posters

If you want to brighten up your bedroom, one idea is to put up some of the colourful posters sold by the wildlife and environmental organisations. Track some down through the organisations listed on pages 86 to 90. You can also buy many other things for your room through their catalogues.

57

How Green is Your Home?

There are always more changes you can make in the way you live which will help to protect the Earth. Now that you have had a good look around your home, try this quiz to find out how your household is doing at the moment.

1 Do you or your family collect any of the following for recycling?
  ✓ a newspapers
  ✓ b aluminium cans
  ✓ c glass bottles or jars
  ✓✓ d plastics
  ✓ e clothes

2 Are any of the following insulated?
  ✓ a roof
  ✓ b water tank
  ✓ c doors (with draught-proof strips)
  ✓ d windows (with draught-proof strips)

3 What kind of deodorants are used in your home?
  ✓ a roll-on or stick
     b aerosol
  ✓✓ c none

4 When you are the last to leave a room, do you leave the light on
     a always
  ✓ b often
  ✓✓ c never

5 If your household runs a car, does it
  ✓ a run on unleaded petrol?
     b run on leaded petrol?
  ½✓ c run on diesel?
  ✓✓ d have a catalytic converter?
  (Score ✓✓✓✓ if you have no car at all)

6 When you make a short journey, do you prefer to
  ✓✓✓ a walk or cycle?
     b ask somebody to take you by car?
  ✓✓ c use public transport?

7 Does your milk come in
  ✓✓ a glass bottles which are returned to the milkman?
     b cardboard cartons?
     c plastic bottles?
     d glass bottles which are thrown away?

8 Is your kettle
  ✓ a clean inside?
    b 'furred' up?
  ✓ c a model with an automatic 'off' switch?

9 Are your egg boxes
    a clear plastic?
  ✓ b cardboard?
    c polystyrene foam?
  ✓✓ d any of the above but returned to the shop?

10 Is the room temperature in your home
  ✓✓ a Under 18°C (65°F)?
  ✓ b 18–21°C (65–70°F)?
    c over 21°C (70°F)?

11 Are your packets of loo rolls labelled
  ✓✓ a 100% recycled paper?
  ✓ b partly recycled paper?
    c no mention made of recycled paper?

12 Are your vegetables bought
  ✓✓ a loose?
    b pre-packed?

13 What type of bags are used for shopping?
  ✓✓✓ a cloth/basket
  ✓ b reused plastic (old ones)
    c new plastic (collected at the checkout)

14 Are spray cans used?
    a yes
  ✓✓ b no

15 Which do you usually have?
    a a bath
  ✓ b a shower

16 How many electrical kitchen appliances do you have?
    a 10 or more
  ✓ b 5–9
  ✓✓ c less than 5

17 If your household has a washing machine, is it used for a full load
  ✓✓ a always?
  ✓ b usually?
    c rarely or never?

18 Do you eat fast food and takeaways
    a often?
  ✓ b rarely?
  ✓✓ c never?

19 Does your household use paper towels or napkins
    a often?
  ✓ b rarely?
  ✓✓ c never?

20 Do you think your home is well protected from draughts?
  ✓ a yes, fairly
  ✓✓ b yes, very
    c no

Count up the number of ticks you have scored and see where you fall on this scale.

0–13 Well, there's a long way to go yet in your household!
14–25 You're turning a pale shade of green . . .
26–37 Getting greener . . .
38–49 Definitely on the green side. Well done, but don't stop trying!

AT SCHOOL

If you and your family can do so much to help solve problems such as Acid Rain and the Greenhouse Effect, imagine how powerful hundreds of green consumers can be if they work together at school. And if all schools were to behave in the same way, the results would be dramatic.

'Greening' your school—whether in the choice of pens and paper you use or the way your school meals are prepared—is a step-by-step process. First you need to find out what is happening at the moment in and around the building—how much electricity is used, how much paper is thrown away for instance. Then you have to consider what can be changed and particularly what *you* can change, so that less damage is caused to our environment. Saving electricity and cutting down on the rubbish are important but there are dozens of other things too. Finally, you need to tell as many people as possible what you have discovered and what action you are taking.

School Environmental Audit

Now, for once, you can set a test for the school instead of the other way round! An audit means a detailed examination and the School Environmental Audit is your means of finding out how 'green', or more likely 'ungreen', your school is at the moment and what improvements can be made. Over the next few pages we give a suggested plan of action which you can use as a basis for your own audit.

The audit doesn't have to be done all at once. It could stretch over a term or even a year. It is important, though, once you've gathered your facts, to go back again to investigate the same issues at a later date. This way you can check whether, and by how much, things have changed.

You'll want to ask many questions of the adults in the school as well as the pupils but don't be downcast if few people know the answers at first. It is very valuable to discover how many people who *should* know what is going on around them, don't. Also, your questions may spark their interest in helping to protect the Earth.

In many schools decisions such as which cleaning liquids are used, what sort of furniture is bought or how the food is prepared, are not taken by the head teacher but by the local authority. So no one at the school may know, for instance, whether you are sitting at tropical hardwood desks. And your school may not easily be able to change away from strong bleaches or switch to recycled loo paper. Your surveys will reveal what the position is and perhaps some suggestions for buying 'green' goods can be made to the local authority.

Six steps to action

1   Approach the teacher you think will be most interested and helpful—probably your class teacher if you are at primary school, otherwise a subject teacher or your form tutor. They might let the audit be organised in class time and they should be able to help you with the questionnaires and perhaps find out more information than you are able to.

2   The audit is best conducted by a group, or several groups, of pupils. Decide how many investigators (auditors) will be involved and in how many groups. They could come from one class, one year or from the whole school. Each group will need a co-ordinator to work with other group co-ordinators to put all your discoveries together.

3   Look through the next few pages and decide how closely you want to follow our plan of action and whether you have any additions to make. The more you do the better because you can only tell how 'green' a school (or any other organisation) is by looking at everything it does. If you only have time for a few sections, however, your investigations will still be very useful.

4   Make sure that everybody is aware of the issues covered in the first part of the book. You will be trying to find out how much each issue is affected by what happens in and around the building.

5   Work out a timetable—how long it should take to complete each section and a date by which the whole audit will be finished.

6   Agree on what you will do with the audit once it is finished. It will be extremely useful to all sorts of people and they can learn a great deal from it. You could give copies to friends, other teachers and adults, school governors. Perhaps also the local authority and the local newspaper. You might also be asked to talk about it—either to a class or even the whole school.

Preparing the environmental audit

Your aim should be to produce a report which, when all the sections are clipped together, gives as clear a picture as possible about the current position in your school. So, for certain issues it is important not only to show how many people do one thing and how many another (e.g. how many people use throwaway pens and how many use long-lasting, refillable pens) but what percentage are already being 'green' and what percentage are not. A good way to do this is by drawing pie charts, bar charts etc. Then you can easily see how much room there is for improvement and check later whether there has been any change.

For some of our suggested investigations you will need to draw up a questionnaire for other pupils and/or staff. For *The Classroom*, for example, you would need to ask:

Do you use ☐ throwaway pens?
☐ refillable pens?
☐ neither?

Do you use a ☐ battery powered calculator?
☐ solar powered calculator?
☐ neither?

What sort of bag do you bring to school?   ☐ a long-lasting bag? (e.g. cloth or nylon)
☐ a throwaway plastic?
☐ neither?

On other issues you may have to ask questions of members of staff—the cleaners, the cooks, the caretaker or the head teacher, for example. Ask the adult who is helping you with the audit to check that you approach the right people, organise the time to see them and write down your questions beforehand so that you don't miss anything out. Also make sure they will not be asked the same questions by another group of auditors. Remember, too, that you are not trying to catch anyone out but are aiming to excite them about your audit and work with them to make your school as green as possible.

To give you some ideas about what your finished report could look like, we have produced a sample on pages 64 and 65. Be sure to leave room for your conclusions and suggestions, both at the end of each section and as a rounding-up piece at the end of the whole audit.

First things first

Aim Before looking at individual rooms and activities it is worth thinking about a few general points to see how aware people are of the issues.

- Does the school have any special guidelines, or one person particularly responsible for working to help the environment? Very few schools have either, but if yours does, we would love to hear from you!

- Since the issues in this book cover every area of our lives you can expect to hear about them in many different lessons. You could list over a period of time how often they are mentioned and in which lessons. Do you feel you learn enough about them or would you like to know more? What do other pupils think?

- Survey a group of pupils and staff to find out whether they can explain, in simple terms, Acid Rain, the Greenhouse Effect and the hole in the ozone layer.

- Is your school library or class bookshelf well stocked with interesting and up-to-date books and periodicals on the various environmental issues? And do you sometimes watch videos about them too? You could start a list of any particularly good books or films you think the school should have.

- Does your school belong to any environmental organisations such as Friends of the Earth, Greenpeace and the World Wide Fund for Nature (originally called the World Wildlife Fund)? Do pupils take part in any special projects such as sponsored fund raising, clearing litter or perhaps helping to set up a nature trail?

- Do any pupils and members of staff belong to environmental organisations themselves?

School Environmental Audit

(This is only an example and does not cover everything you may be able to find out.)

THE CLASSROOM

Date: 22 April 2001
Room name(s)/number(s): Class 6
No. of people surveyed: 28

AIM: To find out how many things in the room may contribute to environmental problems when made, used or thrown away.

1 Using several <u>throwaway plastic pens</u> rather than one refillable pen creates more rubbish and wastes plastic and the energy needed to make the pens.

Number of pupils with throwaway pens   20
refillable pens   2
neither   6

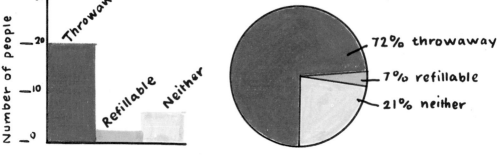

2 <u>Calculators</u> may run on batteries, which take a lot of energy to make and can cause pollution when thrown away, or run on solar power, which is non-polluting.

Number of pupils with battery calculators   11
solar-powered calculators   12
neither   5

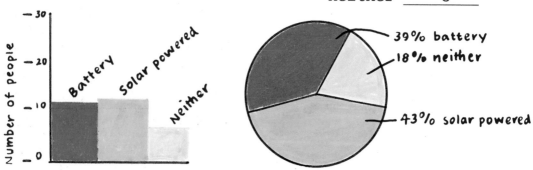

3 Of all the textbooks, notebooks etc used in the classroom,   all _____

none _____✓_____

some _____   are labelled as being made from recycled paper.

4 Ways of saving paper include: Using both sides. Not printing out more than you need to from your computer. Writing small!

5 Number of pupils using

long-lasting school bags (e.g. cloth, nylon) ___10___

throwaway bags ___16___

other ___2___

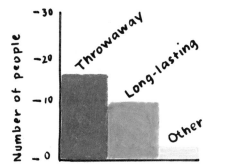

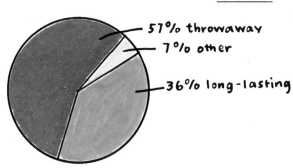

6 Tropical hardwoods, which can contribute to tropical deforestation, may be used for making desks, chairs, blackboards, doors, window frames.

In our school they are used for: Head teacher's study door.

Conclusions and suggestions: In general we found that fewer people use the more 'environment-friendly' alternatives.

It may be difficult to get most people to switch to refillable pens, but solar-powered calculators are more convenient to use - and much cheaper to run.

We felt we needed much more information on recycled paper. We have asked whether the whole class - possibly even the whole school - could switch to text books and notebooks made from recycled paper.

Plastic bags are a waste if only used once. We are telling people to use their bags more often, or suggesting they switch to long-life bags.

We had to look fairly hard to find things made from tropical hardwoods, but the Head wasn't pleased when we discovered her study door was made from mahogany!

Where things have already been made from tropical hardwoods it obviously makes no sense to throw them away. But if they are replaced, tropical hardwoods should not be used.

The Classroom

Aim To find out how many things used in the classroom, from paper to furniture, may contribute to environmental problems when made, used or thrown away. Survey as many different classrooms as you can—and don't forget other teaching areas if you have them.

- List all the different work materials you can find—paper, pens, pencils, glue, sticky tape etc—and try to find out how much of each is bought for the school each term. Can you think of any ways to use less?

- Using several *throwaway plastic pens* rather than one refillable pen creates more rubbish and wastes the plastics and energy needed to make the pen. How many people (including teachers) use throwaway pens and how many use refillable pens?

- Are *calculators* solar powered? If not then the batteries may cause pollution when thrown away (and the batteries take a lot of energy to make). Find out how many of each type are used.

- Are any of your *notebooks or text books* made from recycled paper? Is recycled paper used in any other way?

- Note some of the ways your class could use paper less wastefully (such as always writing on both sides, not printing out more than you need to when working on a computer, and using the back of old computer paper for rough work).

- What sort of *bags* do people bring

to school? Strong, long-lasting bags or disposable plastic carriers?

- Are you able to find out what sort of wood has been used to make your *desks, chairs* (and even your *blackboards* if you have wooden ones)? Has tropical hardwood been used? If you are able to find out who buys the furniture you could ask them whether they have ever thought about what kind of wood they are buying.

Food and drink

Aim To find out whether energy and packaging are wasted. The kitchen is obviously an important place to investigate but if you have a Home Economics room you can ask some of these questions there too. If no food is cooked in your school but meals are delivered from outside, you may have to direct your questions to the suppliers.

- Have any steps already been taken to save energy and packaging? If so, what—and when?

- What type of *cooker* is used at school? Gas? Electricity? Oil-fired? Gas is usually the most energy efficient. (If you are not in a city or large town, however, gas may not be available.)

- Are most foods bought in large packets? Make a list of those that are and of any that are not. Do the kitchen staff feel more could be bought in this way? Do any

foods come in individual portions (e.g. salt, pepper, butter, jam)? If so, they are very wasteful of packaging.

- To give an idea of the amount of *packaging* thrown away in the kitchens you could try to find out how much of certain foods is ordered each week or month. Then ask if you can weigh one each of the empty tins, boxes, bags etc. and multiply the answer by the number used in a week or a month to find out the total weight of packaging thrown away in the same period. (If possible, try to make a comparison with a larger container.)

- Are *leftovers* and other food waste recycled rather than simply thrown away? Perhaps some is fed to school pets, or used for compost in the grounds, or collected and used for pig feed. If not, would this be a possibility?

especially about the materials in which their food is wrapped. Here are some ideas:

What do their sandwiches come in (foil, plastic film, plastic bags, paper, or—the best option—reusable containers such as a tupperware box)? If they are allowed to bring drinks, are they in cartons, plastic throwaway bottles, cans, re-usable containers? How many individually wrapped items do they have (e.g. crisps, cheese biscuits, cakes, chocolate, pies)?

- *Vending machines*. If your school has one of these, work out how many different items are bought each day. What happens to the litter. Is there a bin nearby and a notice on the machine about litter?

- *Packed lunches*. Find out how many people bring these and compare the answer to the number of people eating school dinners. There are many questions you can ask those who bring their own—

- Does the school's *milk* come in returnable glass bottles?

- *Fridges and freezers* contain CFCs in their insulation and cooling system. They therefore contribute to the holes in the ozone layer. If your fridges are old there may be plans to change them. If so, recommend that new models with a reduced CFC content are purchased. Also check what will happen to the old equipment. Will it be sent away to have the CFCs removed from the cooling system and recycled—or will it simply be dumped, in which case the CFCs will finally escape?

The Grounds

m Huge areas of land are given over
school grounds, playing fields and
on and they offer great chances to
courage wildlife. Even if your
hool has little space, there is always
mething that can be done. The aim
to make the space as hospitable as
ossible for plants, animals, birds and
sects.

Can you calculate the area of your
school grounds and work out how
much is taken up by buildings,
how much by car parks, how
much by playgrounds etc., where
there is little room for wildlife?

Find out who looks after the
grounds and ask them whether
they would like to do more for the
wildlife. Do they know where to
go for advice? Your local wildlife
trust would be a good place to
start.

- Are chemical fertilizers, pesticides
  or herbicides used on the grass,
  trees or shrubs? How often? You
  might be able to ask a teacher if
  they can find out whether any of
  these chemicals are particularly
  harmful to wildlife. (Reference
  books like our own *Green Consumer Guide* and *C for Chemicals*
  by Michael Birkin and Brian Price
  should tell them.) Don't forget the
  chemicals used in pools and
  ponds.

- How many species of plants, animals, birds and insects can you
  find? Of the trees and shrubs, do
  you know which ones are indigenous (have always grown in this
  country)? Exotic plants from distant countries are often not popular with native wildlife since they
  do not provide the food it needs.

- Does your school grow any fruit or vegetables? If so, are they grown organically? Some schools have space for pupils to plant their own garden. If yours does, try gardening organically (see page 80). You might also like to see what happens if one area is left uncultivated. List the changes that take place in that area over the course of a term or longer.

- Do the loos have recycled pape Can you find out how much used in a term and a school ye

- Do you dry your hands on tow which are sent away to the laund and reused or on disposable pap towels?

Cleaning

Aim Since so many cleaning materials are now available which are less damaging to the environment, it is worth finding out whether your school has switched to any of them yet. Remember to check the Staff Room, the Art Room and the Home Economics room if you have them, as well as investigating what products are used by the cleaning staff.

- Try to list all the different things used and, following The Kitchen section earlier in this book, note any problems associated with them (e.g. spray cans).

Can you find out whether the person who stocks the cleaning cupboards knows about environmental problems and whether they have already decided to switch away from, for example, spray cans?

Are strong, reusable cloths used or disposable ones? How many of each are used every month?

Rubbish

Aim Every day, the school will throw away large quantities of rubbish. You could be looking for ways to reduce waste and to recycle as much as possible.

Try to find out how many bins or bags of rubbish the school produces each week.

If you can, sample a few rubbish bags and see how much is paper, how much is plastic, how much is metal and how much is glass. (It's a good idea to wear gloves if you're doing this!) Which material takes up the most space and which weighs the most? (You could also do this test on a classroom waste-paper basket.)

- Can you suggest ways to cut down on the amount of rubbish the school creates?

- Is any of the waste collected for recycling? Paper or glass perhaps? Ask other pupils, their parents and the staff whether they would be willing to bring in waste materials for recycling. If enough say yes, suggest to the head teacher that a recycling scheme is started and suggest how it might work.

- Make a list of the things that could be recycled but are not. And those which could be re-used e.g. plastic containers. Also suggest *how* they could be re-used.

- Litter is often a problem where there are lots of people. Are you frequently reminded about it and are litter pick-ups organised? How often? Can you think of ways to stop people dropping litter?

- You could select a patch of your school grounds and count how many pieces of litter appear on it over a week or a month. Compare it to a similar patch of nearby street or park.

Travelling

Aim Since you probably make at least 400 trips to or from school every year, and since transport is one of the key environmental issues, finding out how everyone gets to school is especially important. There is often not much choice in the matter. If you don't live within walking distance, and if there is no school bus or reliable public transport, then you probably travel by car, which is one of the most environmentally damaging ways to get about.

- You might like to carry out two surveys, one for staff and one for pupils. Staff tend to live further away and a higher percentage of them are therefore likely to travel by car.

- Where does each person live and how far do they travel every day, counting the trips both to and from school?

- How does each person travel? By

car, bus, train, bike, foot? Are the able to choose between differer forms of transport? If so, what? they come by car, how mar people are usually in it?

- From the answers, you can wor out the total distances covered t each different method of transpo and the percentage of people wh use each one. What is the order popularity? Pages 18 to 21 will te you which forms of transpo cause the most and the lea damage to the environment.

- One way to reduce the effects car travel is to share the journe with as many people as possibl Your questionnaire answers w show you how many cars car only one passenger, how mar carry two etc. You might also find people who live in the same area who could start to travel by car together.

What percentage of car travellers come in a car which a) uses unleaded petrol? b) has a catalytic converter?

Take a look at how well your school is served by public transport. How close are the nearest bus stops? Could things be improved for pedestrians and for cyclists by creating new crossings and cycle lanes? If you think you have some good suggestions to make, pass them on to your local authority and ask for their reaction.

Saving energy and water

Aim Large groups of people in large buildings can do a great deal to cut down on Acid Rain and the Greenhouse Effect by cutting down on the amount of energy they use, and they can help on other problems by saving water. So it is important that your school does as much as possible.

- Try to find out how much the school's electricity bill is every year, and the gas and oil bills too, if you have them.

- The electricity bill will tell you how

many units the school has used over a few months. Britain's power stations give off about 10 grams of sulphur and 3 grams of nitrogen oxides, both of which cause Acid Rain, for every unit of electricity produced. They also create 1 kilogram of carbon dioxide (the main Greenhouse gas) for every unit. (1 kilogram is enough to fill 20 party balloons!) From these figures you can work out the school's contribution to Acid Rain and the Greenhouse Effect. And if you manage to cut back on the units used you can tell by how much the pollution has been reduced.

- If the bills can be reduced then it means that energy is being saved. Perhaps the school could set itself a target for cutting the bills. It would be up to you to suggest some ways of saving energy and to excite everyone else so that the whole school takes part.

- Most important in terms of saving energy is to have the school well insulated. Try to find out whether the roof, walls and pipes are insulated. Also whether any of the windows are double-glazed.

- Fluorescent lights use less electricity than ordinary light bulbs. How many fluorescent lights do you use and how many ordinary ones? Are there more than are really necessary?

- If you think the classrooms get too hot sometimes, perhaps the heating could be turned down rather than the windows opened.

- Suggest as many ways as possible of saving energy. Are doors left open in winter? Are lights left on in unused rooms and are the fridges in the kitchens kept full? (More energy is used when the fridge has little in it, and also when it needs defrosting.)

- It is important to save water too. Try to find out whether steps have already been taken to do this. Your school may have a meter which measures how much water is used. If so, you could launch a campaign for saving water and cutting down the bills to run alongside your energy-saving programme. Watch out for taps dripping in the washrooms and hosepipes left running in the grounds.

The Neighbourhood

Aim Your school is part of the community and it affects the people living nearby. Try to find out how. Here are some suggestions.

- Are there queues of cars blocking the road and slowing down the traffic when pupils are brought to and picked up from school?

- Are there enough litter bins and are they used? Or is the area around the school always untidy?

- You could carry out a small survey of local residents to find out how they feel about your school and whether they have any suggestions to make.

- Do you know how old the school buildings are? If they are fairly new you may find some local people who remember what was on the land before.

- Are there factories in or near your area? They won't be part of the school environmental audit but another time you could ask to visit them and find out what they are doing and then produce a list of questions for them too.

MAKING AND DOING

Apart from finding out about 'how to be green' at home and at school, there are many other things you can do which can be a lot of fun.

Be a green detective

Environmental detection involves finding out as much as possible about what is going on in the environment around you. That's essential—we have to know what's really happening before we know what needs changing.

You may already have been investigating, for instance, the wildlife in your school grounds or the pollution caused by you and your friends travelling to and from school. But here are a few more ideas.

Acid drops
In recent years, regular checks on acid rain have been organised by WATCH —the young person's section of the Royal Society for Nature Conservation. (See page 87 for the address.) The checks went on all over Europe, and produced vital information for scientists. They have used a simple kit, collecting the rain water in a plastic bag that has an 'indicator strip' in it. If the rain is acid, the strip changes colour. Matching it with a colour card shows *how* acid the water is.

There is a bit more to it, though, i[n] terms of recording the information You need to note things like win[d] direction, any polluting factories [or] chimneys nearby, and other detail[s] The whole process is clearly explaine[d] by WATCH.

If you would rather do the testing o[n] your own, you can get an Acid Dro[p] Test kit from Roopers Ltd, PO Box 8[2] Tunbridge Wells, Kent TN3 8BZ.

Bottle and can banks
Find out whether there are any bottl[e] banks and can banks in your area an[d] if not write to your local council askin[g] *why* not. If there are banks but yo[u] notice that they are overflowing mos[t] of the time, ask whether there ar[e] plans to have them emptied mor[e] often. If the council itself doe[s]

not operate the banks someone there should be able to tell you who to write to instead.

How green is your supermarket?

If you have to help with the shopping use the opportunity to check up on your supermarket. Here are some things to look out for.

- If the shop has been built outside town, can it be reached by public transport or by a special bus laid on by the supermarket? If not, then the supermarket is not helping people who do not own a car, or who prefer to travel by public transport.

- Again, if the supermarket is outside town, have new trees and shrubs been planted? This will help to protect and encourage wildlife in the area.

- Are organic fruit and vegetables on sale? If so, how many different varieties? The more the better, although it is not possible for the supermarkets to guarantee what they will have on sale at any one time.

- Can you find other items labelled 'organic'?

- Are the egg boxes plastic or paper pulp? If both, which is used most?

- How many different labels can you find which appear to mean that one brand is less damaging to the environment than another? Some examples are: *environment-friendly, ozone-friendly, CFC-free, recyclable, made from recycled materials, cruelty-free, mercury free* (on batteries), *phosphate free* (on detergents), *PDCB-free* (on lavatory cleaners). The fact that there are so many different labels causes considerable confusion amongst shoppers who want to buy the least harmful brands. Just because something is CFC-free, for example, doesn't mean that it causes no other problems. (It may be wasteful of packaging.) We think the answer is to have one set of standards, decided by experts, and a 'green' label to show shoppers which items have been approved.

- Can you spot obvious examples of over-packaging?

If you visit more than one supermarket you can compare one with another. And do write to tell the managers the results of your survey. Things will only get better when they know that we really care.

How green are your neighbours?
You can try out the 'How Green is Your Home?' questionnaire (page 58) on other people in your family—grandparents, aunts and uncles. Also on neighbours, if you know them well. You might be surprised at how pleased they are to discover what they can do to be green consumers.

What can you do without?
You will have realised by now that everything we do or buy has some impact on our environment, whether helpful or harmful. We, and those who make the things we buy, use electricity and other forms of energy. That contributes to pollution (see pages 16–17). We use up natural resources. We create waste. So, whenever possible, think about buying less, or not buying at all, before you start to look for the 'greenest' purchase.

Start by making a list of the things you feel you could never give up. Then make a list of things you could cut down on or give up entirely. Next you could draw up a checklist for everyone else in your family to fill in. It might start like this:

crisps and nuts □ could not do
without
□ could cut down on
□ could give up

and include bread, canned fizzy drinks, sweets, air fresheners, milk, kitchen rolls, bubble bath, tinned pet food, eggs, washing-up liquid, electric blankets, new clothes, batteries.

78

You may find you all agree on certain things and could start to put your answers into practice.

Recycling

If you want to set up recycling schemes with a group of friends you could start by telephoning your local council (or your local branch of Friends of the Earth, if you have one) to find out which materials are collected in your area. They might include plastics and batteries as well as glass, cans and paper. It is sometimes difficult to find someone at the council who can give you the answers, but keep trying. If you can't get through on the telephone, try writing.

Penny a Can—recycling aluminium
In Britain we get through over 7 *billion* canned drinks a year and almost half of them are made entirely from aluminium. You can tell whether or not a can is aluminium by placing a magnet against the side of the can and if it *doesn't* stick then you've got aluminium. Page 30 explains why you will be

helping the environment if you work towards recycling more aluminium. But did you know you might also be paid 1p for every can you collect? The Aluminium Can Recycling Association, ALUCAN (address on page 88), advises on collection schemes and suggests a number of things for you to do.

1. Contact them and they will register you as an official collector. They will send you collection bags and leaflets.
2. Find other people—including friends and neighbours—to become Collection Agents.
3. Set yourself a target. Give your collectors their own targets and decide who gets the money. Think about giving it to a charity.
4. Distribute the bags and leaflets sent by ALUCAN to each of your collectors and make sure they know where they can store the cans. They will soon take up a great deal of space.
5. ALUCAN will give you a list of companies in your area which will pay you for the cans. You can also look them up in *Yellow Pages* (copies printed after mid-1989) under 'Waste Reclaimers' or 'Recycling'. If you are collecting really large numbers of cans, the company may even help you with transport.

Don't forget, incidentally, to put the ring pull inside the cans. Ring pulls are all aluminium, even if the can itself is not. So you can collect them separately and fill up some of your empty aluminium cans. Those cans which are not made of aluminium can go in the nearest can bank. These are often near bottle banks.

Collecting paper

As well as collecting paper at home and in the local neighbourhood, you could arrange for parents and other pupils to bring their paper to your school. Exercise books and file paper are particularly good for recycling. It is also possible to recycle paper from magazines and newspapers but find out first whether your local waste paper depot takes them. Not all do.

Some types of paper are more suitable for recycling than others, as the chart shows you.

Recommended for Recycling	Not Recommended for Recycling
Exercise books	Coloured paper (including pale colours)
White file paper	
Photocopying paper	Fax paper
Typing paper	Carbon paper (used in typewriters)
Newspapers*	
Magazines*	Glossy paper
Cardboard*	Papers with glue (e.g. envelopes)
	Books with glue down the spine (e.g. telephone directories)

*Check first whether your local depot will accept it.

(This list has been compiled by Friends of the Earth and SustainAbility)

Making a wildlife garden (organic of course!)

Has anyone ever said you've got 'green fingers'? It usually means you're brilliant at growing plants but it could also be applied to gardeners who protect the environment and allow wildlife to flourish.

If you want to set up a wildlife patch at home, in a friend's garden or at school, here are some ideas to start you off.

- Don't use chemical fertilizers, or pesticide sprays. Nature provides its own pest-killers, but if you use chemical sprays you kill these too. By leaving the pests alone, you're providing dinner for other visitors. If you have greenfly (aphids), ladybirds will arrive to eat them. If you have slugs, hope for toads (or hedgehogs) to feast on them. If you have snails, thrushes will fly to your aid. And the caterpillars munching holes in your leaves will attract bluetits—or turn into butterflies.

- Make a compost heap (page 81). This way, your garden can be fed without chemical fertilizers and a compost heap is a better way of disposing of leaves, grass cuttings etc. than a bonfire.

- Grow flowers like the poached egg plant among your vegetables. They attract insects such as the hoverfly which eat greenfly. (A hoverfly can eat a thousand greenfly in its short lifetime!)

- Ask whether you can dig a small pond. This will attract insect-eating frogs and toads. (Don't add fish—they eat frog spawn.) If you are very lucky, you may also find that dragonflies and even newts arrive.

- Leave a small clutter of sticks and logs in a corner, as a home-from-home for hedgehogs.

Plant a few berry bushes to bring in the birds, along with sunflowers and teasels which produce a great many seeds. A cheap way to build up a variety of plants and bushes is to ask friends for cuttings from their gardens.

Herbs such as sage, thyme and mint are not only tasty in cooking but they attract bees too.

- Make butterflies welcome. They would be perfectly happy with a lush crop of nettles, not to mention dandelions and goldenrod, but your neighbours might be less happy if those fast-growing weeds start spreading. Instead you might offer the butterflies buddleia, lilac, michaelmas daisies, and honeysuckle.

- Low-growing greenery will encourage a variety of beetles, which eat smaller pests.

- If there is room for a patch of long grass you might even get some grasshoppers.

If you get very interested in wildlife gardening there are many books which will give you detailed suggestions for what to grow and how. So will groups like the Royal Society for Nature Conservation and the popular National Centre for Organic Gardening (address on page 89 under HDRA).

Making a compost heap
Instead of throwing out the vegetable peelings and apple cores from your kitchen, start a compost heap if you have a garden. The simplest way is to toss vegetable waste from the kitchen and garden waste into a hole in the ground until it has mostly rotted. But don't swamp the heap with grass cuttings. Mix them with large weeds and perhaps shredded newspaper.

If it all starts to get seriously smelly, fit your compost into a special container or even an old dustbin with a lid. Make sure that there are holes in the top and bottom, for drainage and air circulation.

Window boxes
If you don't have the use of a garden you may like to set up a window box. Although you won't get newts and

hedgehogs, you should find if you plant flowers such as marigolds and snapdragons that butterflies will visit.

Bird tables
You can always do more for birds. As well as growing food for them in the garden you can put up a bird table. Be careful, though, where you put it—it can become a cafeteria for hungry cats! One idea is a hanging table, slung from a tree branch, so that the birds can see a cat climbing up. Birds will be pleased with many kinds of table scraps, along with proper wild bird food. Hang net bags of nuts from branches or from a clothes line and watch the bluetits and their relatives perform acrobatic miracles.

Resign yourself, though, to the fact that another acrobat—the grey squirrel—may get the idea that this free lunch is intended for it.

Green ideas

If you want to make other people aware of their effect on our environment, and encourage them to be green consumers, there are many things you can do. Here are two of them.

Making a shopping bag
This is a good present for the shoppers in your family since it means that they won't need the throwaway bags given to them in the shops.

You could make a bag from old cloth or other materials which would otherwise be thrown out—and if you use plain material there is plenty of scope for decoration. But do make sure that whatever you use it is strong enough to last, and is not too bulky, so that it is easy to carry around.

Shop assistants often try to put each item into a separate bag before it goes into your own bag, which is very wasteful. You have to be quick to stop them but it's worth trying to get into the habit.

Plays and costumes
A good way to wake people up about what is happening to the world is to write and perform a play about one or more of the issues. You could even make the costumes from used packaging. Old paper and plastic bags, egg boxes and bottle tops should come in handy.

Sports and hobbies

Angling
If you fish, you are probably aware of the dangers of carelessly discarded lead weights, old fishing lines and hooks. Swans and other waterfowl often eat the weights or become

...apped in the lines, sometimes with ...tal results. Lead weights under a ...rtain size have now been banned— ...though some anglers continue to use ...em. If you see discarded lines on ...verbanks, take them to the nearest ...tter bin. If you're going fishing your...lf, make sure you take used lines, ...eights and hooks home and dispose ...f them safely.

Birdwatching
...his can be a highly satisfying and, if ...ou record your sightings, a very use...l hobby. The Young Ornithologists ...lub (address on page 88) will send ...ou details of what you can do and ...ow you can help to protect birds. But ...e careful not to disturb them, espe...ally while they are mating or nesting.

Camping
...amping's a great way to enjoy the ...ountryside but do follow these sug...estions:

- Move your tent after a day or so, to avoid killing the grass and other plants under it.

- Don't wash yourself or your dishes in a stream—the stream may not be as clean as you think and you will certainly be polluting it.

- If you stay in a campsite without facilities, dig a hole to use as a lavatory and cover it up when you've finished so that you leave the site as near as possible to the way you found it.

- Dig a similar hole (away from the stream) to pour away dirty water.

- If possible, take a camp stove for cooking. Camp fires are risky in dry areas and leave behind a mess.

- Don't throw things (even biodegradable things such as food scraps) into bushes or streams.

- If you find a site covered in litter, suggest to the owner that a bin (or more bins) is provided.

Model making and painting
If you make models or paint, you probably use glues, paints, varnishes and brush cleaners. Most of these contain chemicals called solvents which give off potentially dangerous vapours. These vapours cause smog in cities and damage to trees.

You can help by:

- Not buying more than you need and using them sparingly.

- Keeping the lid on the can or the cap on the tube whenever you're not using them. This stops the solvents escaping and also makes the glue, paint or varnish last longer.

- Being careful how you dispose of them. Seal the containers and put them in the rubbish bin rather than pouring them down a drain.

And remember to protect yourself by using them in a well-ventilated room.

Photography
Photography is one way of remembering where you have been and what you have done—without taking home with you part of the countryside as a souvenir. But if you enjoy taking photographs and use a modern camera, be careful about disposing of the batteries, especially if yours uses 'button cells'. (See Watches on page 57.) And don't be tempted by disposable cameras which are used for one film and then thrown away. You should also know that the fluids with which your photographs are developed are toxic and that some laboratories may well just dump them down the drain. There are companies, however, which are investigating the possibilities of recycling their developing fluids and other chemicals, which could obviously save them money.

Pets

Before asking your parents for a pet, think carefully about the time and commitment it will require. Pets bring a lot of pleasure, but they are a responsibility too. If you do decide to get one, or if you already have a pet, here are some points to think about.

- *Dogs* need more time and attention than many other pets and hundreds of strays have to be put down every year because their owners have decided they are too much trouble to look after. Also dog fouling in streets and parks is a real problem. Apart from the smell and nuisance it creates when you get it on your shoes, it is a danger to our health. If you get dog muck on your hands or clothes, wash it off immediately.

- *Tins of pet food* create rubbish so recycle them whenever you can or better still, find out from a book about pet care what sort of leftovers or fresh food you can feed your pet.

- *Caged birds* have sometimes been taken straight from the wild and this will have led to the deaths of hundreds of others, either as they were being caught or as they were being transported the long dis

• *Tortoises* were such popular pets at one time, and so many died on their way to us or shortly after they arrived, that in some parts of the world they are almost extinct. It is now illegal to import European tortoises as pets, although they are still brought in from other parts of the world. Since they have such low survival rates it is better to avoid tortoises altogether, unless you're lucky enough to inherit one!

tances to our homes. One reason why some parrots and budgerigars have become endangered species is that so many have been caught for pets. The more expensive and unusual the bird, the more likely it is that the species is under threat. If you do buy a bird, only go to a reputable pet shop or direct to a breeder and even then check that it has been bred in this country.

• Tropical fish should only be bought if they have been bred in captivity (either here or overseas) so that you know you are not reducing their numbers in the wild.

• Asking for an exotic pet may therefore endanger other creatures but if you want to be different, get some *stick insects*. They eat common plants such as ivy and privet, spend much of the day trying to look like twigs and breed like rabbits. They also provide a useful talking point.

Organisations You Can Join

(N.B. JM stands for annual Junior Membership fee)

The Association for the Protection of Rural Scotland (APRS)   14a Napier Road, Edinburgh EH10 5AY. Tel: 031-229 1898. JM: 50p
Works to preserve the countryside and historic buildings of Scotland and is particularly interested in pollution, waste disposal, fish farms, forestry, roads and new buildings. APRS publishes a newsletter and gives awards to schools for successful projects in the local environment. Members are invited to their award ceremonies.

Living Earth Foundation   10 Upper Grosvenor Street, London W1X 9PA. Tel: 01-499 0854. JM: Different fees for different age groups. Send stamped, addressed envelope for details.
The Foundation has major overseas projects on three continents and in the UK works to teach people about the environment. It produces in-

formation for use in schools on such issues as destruction of rainforests; industry and the environment; consumerism; and people, places and plants. It has a rainforest Resource Pack (particularly for schools) and sells posters, cards, T-shirts and other things. Environment days are organised in school holidays and there is a regular programme of fundraising events.

National Trust   36 Queen Anne's Gate, London SW1H 9AS. Tel: 01-222 9251. JM: £7.50
Protects places of historic interest or natural beauty, owning countryside and buildings in England, Wales and Northern Ireland for everyone to see and appreciate. Members receive the National Trust Magazine three times a year and obtain free entry to most National Trust properties. Junior members also receive a special newsletter, Young National Trust. Regional offices organise local activities for young members.

Ramblers' Association   1–5 Wandsworth Road, London SW8 2XX. Tel: 01-582 6878. JM: £6 (free membership to under-16s if parents are members)
Campaigns to protect footpaths and other rights of way and increase access to open country; to defend outstanding landscapes; to encourage people to walk in the countryside. The association is also concerned about the use of pesticides in farming. It does not have ac-

ivities specifically for young members. Members receive a quarterly magazine, the *Ramblers' Yearbook* (a guide for ramblers) and regular information about current issues. Members also enjoy special discounts in some sports shops. There are rambling meetings all year round, including events such as National Family Rambling Day.

Royal Society for the Prevention of Cruelty to Animals (RSPCA)

Causeway, Horsham, West Sussex RH12 1HG. Tel: 0403 64181. JM: £2.50 (individual); £5 for groups

Works for the prevention of cruelty—and the promotion of kindness—to animals. Individual members receive a magazine six times a year, a membership card, certificate, badge, sticker and newsletters. The RSPCA organises many projects including Animal Tracks (this involves going away to learn about one aspect of animal welfare). Other events include sponsored walks and magazine competitions.

WATCH Trust for Environmental Education Ltd

22 The Green, Nettelham, Lincoln LN2 2NR. Tel: 0522 752326. JM: £4 (individual); £6 (family); £10 (3-year individual membership); £14 (3-year family membership)

President is David Bellamy. The organisation aims to increase knowledge of the world about us. It has strong links with schools and takes an active role in conservation projects. Such projects include Frog Watch and Owl Watch. In 1987 it organised the Acid Drops project, involving 20,000 children. The Trust is sponsored by the Royal Society for Nature Conservation and The Sunday Times. Members receive WATCHWORD magazine before every school holiday and three newsletters a year.

Woodcraft Folk

13 Ritherdon Road, London SW17 8QE. Tel: 01-672 6031 or 01-767 2457. JM: Weekly subscription of 20p or more

Works towards a peaceful and safer world, with a particular interest in global issues such as rainforests, local environmental needs, peace issues, development and the Third World. Holds weekly group meetings, and activities include games, craftwork, discussions, local projects and singing. Also regular outdoor activities such as hiking and camping. Age groups are: 6–9, 10–12, 13–15 and 16–20. The Woodcraft Folk Activity Book is available from the organisation and bookshops for £3.99.

World Wide Fund for Nature (WWF)

Panda House, Weyside Park, Godalming, Surrey GU7 1XR. Tel: 0483 426444. JM: £5

One of the largest environmental groups in the country, with sister organisations around the world, WWF encourages the conservation of the natural world. The focus is on environmental issues such as species extinction, loss of habitat, deforestation, energy issues, acid rain, air, sea and land pollution. Members receive a quarterly newsletter, with a youth supplement, a badge and a welcome letter. Conservation and fund-raising events are organised on a local and national level.

Young Ornithologists Club (junior section of the Royal Society for the Protection of Birds, or RSPB)   The Lodge, Sandy, Bedfordshire SG19 2DL. Tel: 0767 80551. JM: £5 (individual); £6 (any number of children living at the same address)
Aims to raise awareness and commitment to nature conservation. Particularly concerned with birds and their habitats. Publishes a bi-monthly colour magazine. Members have free access to RSPB reserves and opportunities to take part in local and national projects and competitions. Every year, the club organises 50 holidays at residential centres throughout Britain and about 100 roadshows. Also numerous local activities based on practical conservation. Schools can become members and take part in relevant activities. This costs £1 per child, with a minimum of 10 children to each group.

Youth Tag Technology Action Group (YT) (supported by Intermediate Technology Development Group) Myson House, Railway Terrace, Rugby CV21 3HT. Tel: 0788 60631. JM: £5
YT has been formed by young people keen to help the poorer countries of the Third World. They raise money to help Intermediate Technology work with communities to design equipment making the most of the resources they have available. They publish four magazines a year and the education office of IT produces a great deal of useful educational material.

USEFUL ADDRESSES

Aluminium Can Recycling Association I-Mex House, 52 Blucher Street, Birmingham B1 1QU. Tel: 021-633 4656.
Educates the public about the benefits of recycling aluminium drinks cans and offers practical assistance to collectors.

Ark Trust   498–500 Harrow Road, London W9 3QA. Tel: 01-968 6780.
Campaigns on general environmental problems, especially relating to human health.

British Trust for Conservation Volunteers (BTCV)   36 St Mary's Street, Wallingford, Oxon OX10 0EU. Tel: 0491 39766.
An important group for people who want to be actively involved in conservation and for advice on local issues. Organise activity holidays (for over-16s only).

Community Recycling Opportunities Programme (CROP)   7 Burner's Lane, Kiln Farm, Milton Keynes MK11 3HA. Tel: 0908 562466.
Aims to encourage people to get together and raise money through recycling.

Council for Environmental Education School of Education, University of Reading, London Road, Reading, Berks RG1 5AQ. Tel: 0734 875123.
Aims to create links between youth organisations and help them learn more about the environment.

Council for the Protection of Rural England (CPRE)   Warwick House, 25 Buckingham Palace Road, London SW1W 0PP. Tel: 01-976 6433.
Campaigns for the protection of the country-side.

Field Studies Council   Central Services, Preston Montford, Montford Bridge, Shrewsbury SY4 1HW.
Tel: Shrewsbury (0743) 850674 or 850997.
Provides courses for schools and families to explore the environment and wildlife around them. The council has ten residential centres around England and Wales, and you can stay either for a couple of days or for a week.

Friends of the Earth (FoE)
26–28 Underwood Street, London N1 7JU. Tel: 01-490 1555.
An environmental action group campaigning on issues ranging from the Greenhouse Effect to tropical deforestation. Also wants to raise awareness of local problems in cities, towns and the countryside. They have a youth section, Earth Action, open to 14- to 23-year-olds.

Greenpeace UK   30–31 Islington Green, London N1 8XE. Tel: 01-354 5100.
Campaigns against the destruction of the natural world by presenting information to the government, backed by scientific research. Also organises non-violent direct action protests. They are very willing to answer questions and give advice to young people who write in with queries.

Groundwork Foundation
Bennetts Court, 6 Bennetts Hill, Birmingham B2 5ST. Tel: 021-236 8565
Organises local environmental projects and welcomes school visits.

Henry Doubleday Research Association (HDRA)   National Centre for Organic Gardening, Ryton-on-Dunsmore, Coventry CV8 3LG. Tel: 0203 303517.
Encourages and researches into organic gardening and farming, and works to save many threatened British seed varieties from extinction.

Marine Conservation Society
9 Gloucester Road, Ross on Wye, Herefordshire HR9 5BU. Tel: 0989 66017.
Conserves the oceans and their inhabitants, from rare corals to basking sharks.

Oxfam   272 Banbury Road, Oxford OX2 7DZ. Tel: 0865 56777.
Encourages people to take an interest in the links between the environment and the developing world, and to help relieve poverty, distress and suffering in every part of the world. Most local activities run alongside the national Oxfam campaigns. These campaigns focus on topics such as relief aid, deforestation and soil erosion.

Soil Association   86 Colston Street, Bristol BS1 5BB. Tel: 0272 290661.
Aims to protect the environment by encouraging organic farming. The association produces an education pack and welcomes all interest from young people.

Tidy Britain Group The Pier, Wigan, Lancs WN3 4EX. Tel: 0942 824620.
Works to control litter in towns and the countryside and produces an education pack for schools, which includes ideas for a general clean up of the urban environment and for improving school grounds. The group also operates an information service for young people who have written in with questions.

Traidcraft plc Kingsway, Gateshead, Tyne and Wear NE11 0NE. Tel: 091-491 0591.
This company sells goods from the Third World such as food, gifts and clothing, making sure that the producers receive a fair price.

Transport 2000 Walkden House, 10 Melton Street, London NW1 2EJ. Tel: 01-388 8386.
Lobbies national and local government for more sensible transport policies. Aims to encourage the use of public transport, to protect the environment and to conserve land and energy.

WASTE WATCH National Council for Voluntary Organisations, 26 Bedford Square, London WC1B 3HU. Tel: 01-636 4066.
WASTE WATCH has been created by the National Council for Voluntary Organisations to organise community-based recycling and reclamation schemes. Events happen within relevant voluntary groups. Details of groups in your area and a guide to recycling for use by local groups are available from WASTE WATCH.

A Dustbin Guide for Schools is available from the Department of Trade and Industry and sponsored by Coca-Cola. It contains Teachers' notes, individual projects on recyclable materials, how to set up collection schemes, games and posters.

Woodland Trust Autumn Park, Grantham, Lincolnshire NG31 6LL Tel: 0496 74297
Cares for and maintains forests and woodlands, often by buying them when they are considered to be endangered. Organises a National Tree Week every year, during which members can participate in activities such as coppicing and tree-planting.

Other Books to Read

If you have enjoyed reading *The Young Green Consumer Guide*, here is a selection of other books which we think are amongst the most interesting and up to date. If you find others which you think should be added to our list, write to us at the address on page 7. We have included at the end a short list of books for younger children.

Non-Fiction

The Food Chain: A game of choice *by Michael Allaby* 1984 (Andre Deutsch 0 233 97681 2)

The Climate Crisis *by John Becklake* (Issues series) 1989 (Franklin Watts 0 86313 946 9) Also in this series, Toxic Waste and Recycling.

Acid Rain *by John Baines* (Conserving Our World series) 1989 (Wayland 1 85210 694 8)

Endangered Wildlife *by Martin Banks* (World Issues series) 1987 (Wayland 0 85078 954 0)

Conserving Rainforests *by Martin Banks* (Conserving Our World series) 1989 (Wayland 1 85210 695 6) Also in this series, The Spread of Deserts, Waste and Recycling.

Animal Rights *by Miles Barton* (Survival series) 1987 (Franklin Watts 0 86313 541 2)

Countryside Under Threat *by Laurie Bolwell and Cliff Lines* (County Leisure Guides) 1986 (Wayland 0 85078 938 9)

The Dying Sea *by Michael Bright* 1988 (0 86313 729 6); Saving The Whale *by Michael Bright* 1987 (0 86313 616 8) (Survival series, Franklin Watts)

The Greenpeace Story *by Michael Brown* 1989 (Dorling Kindersley 0 86318 328 X)

Close to Extinction *by John Burton* (Survival series) 1988 (Franklin Watts 0 86313 730 X)

Air Ecology *by Jennifer Cochrane* 1987 (0 85078 893 5); Animal Ecology 1986 (1 85210 014 1); Land Ecology 1986 (0 85078 891 9); Plant Ecology 1987 (0 85078 911 7); Urban Ecology 1987 (0 85078 894 3); Water Ecology 1987 (0 85078 892 7). (All titles in Project Ecology series, Wayland)

Save Our Planet: An anti-nuclear guide for teenagers *by John Eldridge* 1987 (Magnet 0 416 02512 9)

Pollution and the Environment *by Mary Lean* 1985 (Macdonald Children's Books 0 7500 0019 8)

Atlas of Environmental Issues *by Nick Middleton* 1988 (Oxford University Press 0 19 831674) (also Atlas of World Issues 1988 019 913335 2)

The Gaia Atlas of Planet Management *Norman Myers (General Editor)* 1985 (Pan Books 03 28491 6)

Pollution and Conservation *by Penny Malcolm* (Our World series) 1988 (Wayland 1 85210 362 0)

The Greenhouse Effect and Ozone Layer *by Philip Neal* 1989 (Dryad Press 0 85219 822 1) Also in this series, Disappearing Rainforests, Energy, Power Sources and Electricity, and War on Waste.

Earth's Resources *by Don Radford* (Today's World series) 1983 (Batsford 0 71344 459 2)

Vanishing Habitats *by Simon Noel* (Survival series) 1987 (Franklin Watts 0 86313 592 7)

What is a Rain Forest? *by Philip Whitfield* 1989 (British Museum 0 565 01096 4)

Conserving the Jungles *by Laurence Williams* 1989 (Evans 0 237 51103 7)

Fiction

Awaiting Developments *by Judy Allen* 1988 (Julia MacRae 0 86203 356 X)

Pig in the Middle *by Sam Llewellyn*, hb: 1989 (0 74450 817 7) pb: 1990 (0 74451 420 7) (Walker Books)

Once Upon a Planet *edited by Christina Martinez* 1989 (Puffin 0 14 032179 9)

What On Earth . . .? *edited by Judith Nicholls* hb: 1989 (0 571 15261 9) pb: 1989 (0 571 15262 7) (Faber)

The Plant that Ate the World *by Hugh Scott* 1989 (Faber 0 571 15440 9)

For Younger Children

Where the Forest Meets the Sea *by Jeannie Baker* 1988 (Julia MacRae 0 86203 317 9)

Oi! Get off our Train *by John Burningham* 1989 (Jonathan Cape 0 224 02698 4)

Rainforest *by Helen Cowcher* 1988 (Andre Deutsch 0 233 98266 3)

Trick a Tracker *by Michael Foreman* 1981 (Gollancz 0 575 02975 7)

Adam and Paradise Island *by Charles Keeping* 1989 (Oxford University Press 0 19 279842 1)

Hetty and Harriet *by Graham Oakley* 1981 (Macmillan 0 333 32373 4)

We wish to thank Elaine Elkington, Lynne Parkin (Tameside Libraries and Art Department) and Books For A Change bookshop for their help in compiling this list.

Index

Accidents, 19
Acid rain, 4, 12–13, 74, 76
Aeroplanes, 20
Aerosols, 11, 32–3, 38
ALUCAN, 79
Aluminium, 30, 42, 78–9
  cans, 30, 42, 78–9
  foil, 48
Angling, 82–3
Animals, 6, 15, 26–7
  fur, 54
  pets, 84–5
  testing on, 26

Bags
  school, 66–7
  shopping, 36, 82
Bathroom, 32–5
Batteries, 52–3, 57, 84
Bedroom, 53–7
Beef, 45
Beer, organic, 44
Beeswax polish, 48
Bicycles, 21
Biodegradable, 4, 31
Biomass power, 17
Birds, caged, 84–5
Bird tables, 82
Birdwatching, 83
Bleach, 24, 33–4, 47
Books in schools, 63, 66
Bottle banks, 29, 76–7
Bottled water, 44
Bottles, 28, 29, 38, 43, 44
Brazil, 9, 14, 17
  nuts, 14, 38, 40–1
Bread, 39
Breakfast cereals, 38
Budgerigars, 85
Bulk buying, 36, 38
Buses, 21
Butter, 38
Butterflies, 81, 82

Cadmium, 48, 52–3
Calculators, 66
Camping, 83
Canada, 13
Can banks, 76, 79
Cans, 28, 30, 42, 78–9
Carbon dioxide, 4, 5, 8, 9,
    18, 20, 74
  natural absorption of, 10,
    14

Carbon monoxide, 18
Cars, 4, 18–20, 72, 75
Cassette players, 53
Catalytic converter, 4, 19, 20
Central heating, 51
Cereals see Breakfast cereals
CFCs see
    Chlorofluorocarbons
Chemicals
  in farming, 22
  on school grounds, 69
Chicken, 42
China, 11
Chlorofluorocarbons, 4, 5, 8,
    10–11, 45, 49–50, 68
Classroom, 66–7
Cleaning products, 46–8,
    70–1
Clingfilm, 48
Clothes, 53–5
Coal, 12, 16
Cocoa, 44
Coffee, 44
Compost, 80, 81
Cookers, 49, 67
Cooking oil, 41
Coral, 56
Cotton, 54
Cream, 38
Crisps, 31

Deforestation, 4, 56
Deodorants 32–3
Diamonds, 56
Diesel engines, 18–19
Dioxins, 34
Dishwashers, 50
Dogs, 84
Dolphins, 41–2
Double-glazing, 52
Drinks, 42–4

Ecology, 4
Ecosystem, 4, 7, 14
Eggs, 23, 38–9
  boxes, 39, 77
Electricity, 4, 14, 49
  saving, 9
  school consumption of, 74
Endangered species, 27
Energy, 4, 16–17
  alternative, 16–17
  conservation, 4, 17, 49–50,
    73–4
  efficiency, 4, 17
  renewable, 5, 16–17
Environment, 4
Environmental audit, 60–5
Erosion of soil, 15
Extinction of animals, 15, 27
Exxon Valdez, 25

Fabrics, 53–4
Factories, 75
Factory farming, 23
Farming, 22–3, 54
Fashion, 54–5
Fast food, 44–5
Fertilizer
  artificial, 22
  organic, 23
Fire
  domestic, 51
  lighters, 51
Fish, 13, 25, 41–2
  farming, 41
  tropical, 85
Fishing, 82–3
Fizzy drinks, 42–3
Floods, 9
Flour, 39
Food, 9, 14, 22
  organic, 36–40
  pet, 84
  in school, 67–8

Forests and acid rain, 13
  see also Rainforests
Fossil fuels, 4, 8, 12
Free-range, 5
  eggs, 38–9
  meat, 26, 42
Freezers, 49–50, 68
Fridges, 11, 49–50, 68
Fruit
  juice, 43
  organic, 39, 77
  seasonal, 40
Fuel
  for cars, 19
  for planes, 20
Fur, 54
Furniture, 51–2

Garden
  school, 70
  wildlife, 80–2
Gas, 16, 49
Geothermal power, 17
Glass, 29, 43
Global warming, 9
Gold, 56–7
Greenhouse Effect, 5, 8–10,
  14, 74
Grounds, school, 69–70

Hair conditioner, 34
Health food, 36–42
Hedgerows, 22
Home, 32–57
  Quiz, 58–9
Honey, 40
Hydrocarbons, 18

Ice-cream, 40
Iceland, 17
Ivory, 56

Jewellery, 56
Jungle *see* Rainforest

Kettles, 50
Kitchen, 35–50
  school, 67

Labelling, 77
Laboratory animals, 26
Lavatory *see* Loo
Leftover school dinners, 67
Lifestyle, 6, 78
Litter, 71, 75
Loo
  cleaners, 33
  flushing, 24, 33
  paper, 33–4, 70
  seats, 34
Lorries, 19

Machines in kitchen, 49–50
Meat, 42
  see also Beef, Chicken,
  Turkey
Medicines 15, 34
Mendes, Chico, 40
Metals, 30
Methane, 5, 8
Milk, 38, 68
  bottles, 38
Model making, 83–4
Modern inventions, 6
Montreal Protocol, 11
Motorways, 19
Muesli, 38
Music, 53

National Centre for Organic
  Gardening, 81
Nitrates, 22
Nitrogen oxide, 4, 8, 12, 18,
  74
Nitrous oxides, 5
Non-renewable resource, 5
Nuclear power, 16
Nuclear waste, 16, 25
Nuts, 14, 38, 40–1

Oil, 16, 19
  cooking, 41
  spillage, 25
Organic
  drinks, 44

farming, 5, 23
shopping, 36–42
Organisations,
  environmental, 63
Oven cleaner, 48
Ozone layer, 5, 10–11

Packaging, 28–32, 34, 35–?
  77
  of fruit and vegetables,
  39–40
  of school food, 67
  of sweets, 46
Packed lunches, 68
Painting, 83–4
Paper, 29
  loo, 33–4, 70
  recycling, 79–80
  in school, 66
Parents, 7
Parrots, 85
Pearls, 57
Pens, 66
Personal action plan, 78
PET *see* Polyethylene
  terephthalate
Petrol, 19–20
Pets, 84–5
Phosphates, 22, 24, 47
Photography, 84
Plankton, 10
Plastic, 31
  bags, 36, 67
  buckets, 48
  PET, 43
  washing-up bowls, 48
Plays, writing and
  performing, 82
Polishes, 48
  beeswax, 48
Pollution, 5
  from cars, 18
  from farming, 22–3
  from noise, 53
  from oil spillage, 25
  from sewage, 24–5
  from sugar, 45–6
Polyethylene terephthalate
  (PET), 43
Ponds, 80
Population levels, 7, 14
Posters, 57

Questionnaires, 58–9, 62

Rainforest, 5, 10, 14–15, 5?
Razors, 35

94

ecord players, 53
ecycling, 5, 28, 43, 71,
    78–80
enewable energy, 5
e-usable, 5, 28
iver pollution, 24
oyal Society for Nature
    Conservation, 81
ubbish, 28–31
  school, 71
  see also Waste

chool, 60–74
chool environmental audit,
    60–5
ea level, 9
ewage, 24–5
hampoo, 34
having, 34–5
hells, 57
hopping, 36–46
  bags, 36, 82
howers, 32
itting room, 51–3
lurry, 23
mith, Angus, 12
oap, 35
oil erosion, 15
olar energy, 16
olvents, 83–4
tick insects, 85
ugar, 45

Sugar cane, 45
  energy from, 17
Sulphur dioxide, 4, 12, 74
Supermarkets, 36, 40, 77–8
Sweden, 13, 17
Sweets, 45–6

Takeaway food, 44–5
Tapes, music, 53
Tea, 43–4
Teachers, 7
Third World, 5, 6
Tidal power, 17
Tins, 30
Titanium dioxide, 35
Toilet *see* Loo
Toothpaste, 35
Tortoises, 85
Tortoiseshell, 56
Traffic jams, 19
Trains, 20
Transport, 18–21
  to school, 72
  to supermarket, 77
Travel, 18
Tropical fish, 85
Tropical hardwood, 14, 34,
    48
T-shirts, 55
Tumble driers, 50
Tuna, 41–2
Turkey, 42

Ultra-violet light, 10
Unleaded petrol, 19

Vegetables
  organic, 39, 77
  seasonal, 40

Vending machines, 68

Washing machines, 50
Washing powder, 46–7
Washing-up liquid, 47–8
Waste
  creation, 28–31, 44–5
  disposal, 5, 6
  nuclear, 16, 25
  school, 71
WATCH, 76
Watches, 57
Water, 24–5, 74
  bottled, 44
  filters, 44
Wave power, 16
Weather, 9, 10
Wildlife
  garden, 80–2
  in school grounds, 69
Windmills, 16
Windows, 52
  boxes, 81–2
  cleaners, 48
Wine, organic, 44
Wool, 53–4

Yoghurt, 40
Young Ornithologists Club,
    83

ACKNOWLEDGEMENTS

Our task in writing this book was enormously eased by Douglas Hill, whose energy, insight and humour made the whole process possible—and great fun. And we should also like to thank Tony Ross for his wonderful illustrations, and Ian Craig for his imaginative design.

Others whose inputs helped shape the book include Isabelle Gore of Sustain-Ability, Jackie Gear of the National Centre for Organic Gardening, Steve Bonnist of the Intermediate Technology Development Group, Libby Grundy of the Council for Environmental Education, David Cameron of Books for a Change, and Elaine Gaia and Hania Elkington.

But probably our greatest single debt is to Liz Knights—our Editor—and her colleagues at Victor Gollancz, including Caroline Bingham, Elizabeth Dobson and Chris Kloet. Thank you all.

John Elkington & Julia Haile

PUBLISHERS' NOTE

The paper on which this book is printed is made in Italy at a mill which takes strict precautions to avoid polluting its environment. The pulp used in the paper is oxygen (non-chlorine) bleached, and 15% is made by the mill from waste wood chips, which come from Italian poplar used by local furniture makers—not from tropical hardwoods.

You may well wonder why we have not used recycled paper, as we did in *The Green Consumer's Supermarket Shopping Guide.* One answer is that recycled paper made from waste paper of the sort you might throw away is not yet suitable for printing books with brightly coloured illustrations.

Recycled paper has however been used where the opportunity arose in the production of the book: drafts of the text were printed out on recycled paper, and the typesetter used recycled copier paper for the proofs. And there are other paper products which can and do make effective use of all kinds of waste paper. So, for example, if you are reading a hardback copy of the book there will be recycled paper in the boards under the printed cover, and the cardboard packing in which the books are sent to the bookseller is made from waste paper.